THE LIFE AND LEGACY

of

B.B. King

A MISSISSIPPI BLUES ICON

DIANE WILLIAMS | *Foreword by Dr. London G. Branch*

THE
History
PRESS

Published by The History Press
Charleston, SC
www.historypress.com

Copyright © 2019 by Diane Williams
All rights reserved

Cover photo courtesy of Amile Wilson.

First published 2019

Manufactured in the United States

ISBN 9781467142403

Library of Congress Control Number: 2019948135

*This book is dedicated to my eldest son, James Allen Humphrey,
who lives with the blues every day.*

CONTENTS

CONTENTS

FOREWORD

America has finally begun to respect certain aspects of its own culture. But when the Europeans arrived in the "New World," the developing culture was thought to be inferior to European culture. Art, literature and music was considered low-class and undeserving of the respect that was given to European art, literature and music. White Americans themselves found it difficult to admit that a people of African origin, said to have no intelligence and no soul and to be essentially animal-like, could produce a genre of music that would eventually be recognized as the United States' contribution to the fine arts. Even though it took Americans a while to recognize blues music as art, it did not take Europeans long to catch on, and they soon began acknowledging its contributions. As blues musicians began to travel abroad during the 1920s, many found that their music was readily acceptable by the French and English cultures. At the same time, in America, blues musicians were becoming very popular entertainers in African American juke joints, taverns and blues houses.

African American music had its beginning with the explorative journey of field hollers, primitive songs that were in some cases humming, moaning and using a few words to describe working or living conditions. As stories became longer, complete songs developed. This book is a history of how an important genre of African American music developed from those humble beginnings into a very influential body of literature from which characteristics are present in virtually all American musical genres today.

This is the story of Riley B.B. King and his journey from the cotton fields of Mississippi to the most elegant venues throughout the world. Riley King studied the music of the old musicians, some of whom passed on but made recordings that King could listen to, and others who were still alive who he listened to and studied. King's time in Memphis was very important and was referred at length. Further, this book contains interviews conducted by the author with both old and young musicians who either played with B.B. King or were influenced by his music. The book describes the musical and social conditions under which black musicians worked and lived.

The time has arrived in America for a book to be written about a successful blues musician, and that book can be accepted in academia with the same level of respect as books about European music. As Ray Charles famously said, "Everybody loves the blues." This is demonstrated by the fact that all genres of pop, gospel, jazz and classical music of certain composers use characteristics of it. Here is a book that tells of the life of a great blues musician—his struggles, his failures and his successes. Diane Williams is to be commended for her effort to tell the complete story of a boy from a small town in Mississippi who, through his own talent and tenacity, rose to international prominence and gained the respect of musicians of all genres. The influence of B.B. King has deep roots in the music of many European guitarists and singers, as well as American musicians.

This book is a wonderful introduction to the music and life of a great musician, Riley B.B. King. When you complete it, it is the hope that your knowledge of the blues, especially as played and sung by B.B. King, will inspire you to probe deeply into the world of this great artform.

DR. LONDON G. BRANCH,
musician, instructor, mentor and recipient of the
Governor's Award for Excellence in Mississippi (2019)

ACKNOWLEDGEMENTS

To my two editors, Benjamin Morris, PhD and Susan Marquez; to my roadies and researchers Lena Jones and Brinda Willis, PhD. Special thanks also to Sade Cassie Turnipseed, PhD.; House of Khafre Inc.; Billy Johnson; Highway 61 Blues Museum; Leland, MS; Scott Barretta, who knows a whole lot about the world of blues; Nellie McInnis, who celebrates my creativity every day; Robert Terrell, director of operations, B.B. King Museum; Robert Hill of radio station WRNE in Pensacola, Florida; Leila Salisbury, who put the idea of writing this book on my radar; Craig Gill and the University Press of Mississippi, who wholeheartedly supported the idea of this book; Fellowship Bible Church, my prayer warriors; to my son and encourager Perry Williams; and to my friend Larry D. Williams Sr. and the Pensacola Writer's Retreat in Escambia County, Florida (every writer needs a place to retreat—thank you for the inspirational oceanside bird sanctuary).

Wholehearted gratitude to my dear friend Deborah Rae Wright for traveling with me to a B.B. King concert in San Francisco and sharing the thrill of finding out we were booked at the same hotel in Emeryville where B.B. King and his band were staying. The earthquake we felt late that night in August 2014 was reported at a magnitude of 4.0.

INTRODUCTION

Rileigh B. King (1925–2015), better known as B.B. King, was one of the most accomplished and renowned blues musicians in the world. A consummate musician and singer, King was an encourager, mentor and self-professed ambassador for the blues. Some folks have wondered whether the blues died when he did, although his life's work, as it relates to the blues, lends itself to the preservation of this music. His voice and the sound coming from his guitar are recognized the moment he starts singing and playing.

B.B.'s name was originally spelled *Rileigh* King. Born in Mississippi, he has always called the Delta his home, and he never failed to come back to the place of his roots—the place where his heart beat the loudest: Indianola in Sunflower County. His annual homecoming festivals are celebrated by people from all walks of life, and people continue to honor this gifted gentleman. Indianola was his stomping ground, and the homecoming festival was a sacred place where other musicians felt comfortable being around him. Some were fortunate to be able to proclaim that they performed at the same event where he was showcased.

This book gives a brief account of the life of the King of the Blues, his legacy and perspectives on his character from other blues musicians, with a glimpse of what Magnolia blues (Mississippi blues) has meant to their journey with blues music. The first part of the book is about King himself—a man who left his humble beginnings to travel the world and learn from a variety of experiences. Throughout his life, King sought to treat people right, to care for and encourage others and to promote learning, mentorship, friendship, equality, camaraderie and blues music. He lived with diabetes for more than twenty years of his life, and he died of vascular dementia. Nonetheless, he was loved by all and will never be forgotten.

The second part of the book provides the reader with a few reflections from family relations. Section three recaps interviews with musicians—mostly Mississippians who were impressed by blues music and the work of B.B. King. Each interview lends itself to the history of the blues and to King's legacy. Many of these voices reflect on King's encouragement and kindnesses.

Finally, the book points the reader in a direction where they can learn more about the blues. The Mississippi Blues Trail Curriculum, written by Mark Malone and Scott Barretta, is linked to the Mississippi Arts Commission's website. Similarly, the Blues Curriculum, written by Althea Jerome, is housed on the B.B. King Museum and Delta Interpretive Center's website. Both are resources of which B.B. King would have been proud. Now young people everywhere can learn about the blues and carry on the legacy.

I've had the opportunity to see B.B. King in performance and the great privilege to actually meet and talk with him. The first time I saw the King was during a performance at Thalia Mara Hall in Jackson, Mississippi, in 2001. I was married at the time and the concert was an anniversary gift from my husband. We were seated in the nosebleed section in one of the last few rows of the theater, but even from that far away, the sound of King's guitar, Lucille, sent chills up and down my spine. When King sang, his consummate mastery became something I would always remember. Thalia Mara Concert Hall echoed the blues that night, affirming that we were listening to a king, an ambassador and a trailblazer.

The second time I saw King was during a gathering at the Canton Public Library not long after seeing him in concert. It was an intimate setting with children and their parents who had been invited from the Madison County community. The participants were part of a family reading program. This was a special event that had not been announced to the public. After everyone was gathered, a man walked into the room. He had King's guitar in his hands, and he sat it down in front of the audience as if it belonged to royalty. The children were seated on the floor in front of the guitar, and their parents sat in chairs placed all along the wall. I sat inconspicuously amid the crowd. I had my harmonica-playing performance partner, Oscar Wilson, with me. Oscar loved B.B. King and was hoping to have an opportunity to talk with him. When King walked into the room, he looked around at the children crowded on the floor and said, "Do you know who I am?" The children turned around and looked at their parents for help. The parents, who were all fans of B.B. King, were captivated. They wanted their children to have this opportunity to receive a history lesson. What better way to teach children than to have the legend speak to them directly?

Excited, Oscar burst out with, "Mr. King. Mr. King!" B.B. King politely informed Oscar that he was there for the children. But the look in Oscar's eyes convinced King that he was an earnest fan, so King went ahead and signed one of Oscar's harmonicas.

My third opportunity to see B.B. King was in San Francisco in 2014, when two large celebrity Prevost buses pulled up to the front door of the hotel where I was lodging. It's important to say a word or two about those vehicles—just one of those buses probably cost more than a million dollars. They were filled with King's family members, including his grandson Albert "Mook;" a road manager; eight musicians; and four full-time drivers, who could match any bodyguard in a wrestling match.

The buses were equipped with amenities to give the passengers a home away from home. The buses were considered B.B. King's houses. One was silver and the other was blood red. King rode in the silver bus, while the musicians rode in the beautiful red bus. When asked why King would allow his musicians to travel in what appeared to be the nicer looking of the two buses, Melvin Jackson, one of the musicians, said to me, "Mr. King treated his musicians very well and wanted them to be comfortable."

B.B. King and his band were known for their road tours. That's where they lived, and that's what they loved. That's where their heartbeats connected with the King—on the road and on the stage at least three hundred days a year. He didn't slow down until his health and age made it difficult to keep up with such a grueling schedule. Obviously, with so many days on the road, it was important to not have the driver falling asleep at the wheel. Therefore, two drivers were assigned to each bus. Switching drivers regularly was a strategy that kept the band and crew safe. On the back of the buses were two license tags. One was the tag required by the state of Nevada, and the other one read "B.B. King Worldwide." On the side of the silver bus, the small print read:

King Road Shows
Las Vegas, NV
DOT #618749

As the musicians exited the bus, they were confident that only a few people would recognize their faces, but the small print on the side of the bus was a dead giveaway.

Myron Johnson, King's personal assistant, appeared to be the road manager in charge. It was his responsibility to make sure that everyone was in tune with the schedule. He handled the hotel check-in for everyone and made sure that B.B. King had all the home away from home comforts. On this occasion, they arrived in San Francisco five days early. This gave them enough time to shake off any road weariness so they could enjoy the city. The Hilton Gardens Inn in Emeryville, California, just across the Bay Bridge from San Francisco, was a mainstay for King and his entourage. Because they were on the road most of the year, it was important to have accommodations that met the band's expectations.

The concert was going to take place on Friday, August 22, 2014, at the Warfield Theatre, located at 982 Market Street in San Francisco. The community life surrounding the theater was much different from the comfortable lifestyle of the King and nothing like the Mississippi Delta lifestyle of King's past. All along Market Street you could see and smell the stench of homelessness that rivaled larger cities, such as New York. The people passing through this section of town were jaded by the level of poverty on the streets, with imagery that stood in stark contrast to the businesses and restaurants that flanked the sidewalks. The homeless people used doorways for restrooms in broad daylight, and alcohol and drugs were consumed at night, while broken bottles were scattered along the curb. People, mostly men, were sitting, standing and lying down throughout the streets, and more and more of them were huddling around the BART train station. Two men were digging in a trash can on the corner not far from the theater. While one man was looking for cans to recycle, the other was looking for unfinished and unconsumed food and drink. For him, it was supper time.

As the sky became dark and the hour drew closer to the time of the performance, the homeless people became anxious for a place to sleep. Some were stricken with mental and emotional illness. Some were crippled with hopelessness; some just didn't care and a few still had the ingenuity and creativity to pull a scam or two on an unsuspecting participant. There were no modern conveniences for the people scattered along the landscape of this district, and a sideways glance in any direction would find a man pressed up against a doorway with his back to passersby, relieving himself with his last ounce of modesty and a pound of "I don't care." The air was filled with the blues.

The Warfield Theatre in San Francisco, California. *Courtesy of Diane Williams.*

Yet in a way, this was a perfect backdrop for what was about to take place inside the theater. Blues songs would rise from the stage, and the sound of B.B. King's guitar, Lucille, would resonate in the hearts of his listeners, many of whom had been following King for years. Even the young people in the crowd seemed to be there because they wanted to experience his signature style in action.

The theater itself was unassuming on the outside and designed to resemble a small opera house on the inside, with approximately twenty-three hundred seats. The setting provided the perfect ambiance for an intimate evening with the King. Outside, people stood in two lines—one stretching down one end of Market Street and the other stretching up the other end and around the block. The anticipation and excitement were evident. The crowd represented the diversity of blues aficionados who realized that a career of far more than fifty years of playing the blues would be on stage in concert that night.

The young people standing in line may have only seen the King on YouTube or in a film or heard him on the radio. Some may have heard their parents or grandparents talking about him or singing some of his songs.

Those songs reached way back and were sung from deep within the gut because they were reminiscent of a time when Riley B. King was a child, and his earliest singing echoed the days when his ancestors were slaves. Those early experiences gave King authority to know that the blues songs of old were redemptive salve for sore and aching bones from slaving—that those songs traveled down through time to his mama's sweet singing voice, the voice that he listened to daily while working with her out in the cotton and soybean fields. He also knew that the blues songs of his lifetime represented current events and travails in whatever time they were sung. In 1982, B.B. King donated his collection of seven thousand records to Farley Hall, the music library within the University of Mississippi Blues Archives. That list itself is interesting to browse through for clues about influences on King.

Everyone at the Warfield Theatre had a favorite B.B. King tune. An Englishman standing in line said that his favorite song was "Three O'clock Blues." An African American woman mentioned that "Every Day I Have the Blues" was her favorite. A few hand claps interrupted the conversation, and other people shouted their favorites, such as "Lucille." Some people even swooned and dipped in the night air when someone mentioned "The Thrill Is Gone." An older woman of sixty-one, thought she would amaze the crowd with her recollection. She shouted out, "I'll bet y'all don't remember him singing, 'Nobody Loves Me but My Mother (And She Could Be Jivin' Too!)?'" She even sang a few bars from the song. A camaraderie began to take hold of the crowd as everyone wanted to learn the one song they had not heard before. People became friends standing outside the theater. The bond was created around music and was strengthened by anyone who could hold a tune and sing a line from one of the songs that B.B. King might perform.

The crowd knew that they were going to see a legend, whose metaphorical steam engine's coal bin was filled with embers stoked by eight band members who were dedicated to recreating the legendary sound they had been performing for years. Ernest Vantrease, keyboard player, had been with the King since 2005, after playing with Ray Charles for more than twenty-five years. Seasoned musicianship was an understatement for the staging that took place anywhere King and his musicians performed.

Other members of the band who were known as the King's Men:
Reggie Richards, bass—formerly with Bobby "Blue" Bland
Herman Jackson, drums—formerly with Journey (his brother is Randy
 Jackson of American Idol fame)

Charlie Dennis "Charlie Tuna," guitar—formerly with Bobby "Blue" Bland
Walter Riley King, saxophone and flute (B. B. King's nephew and band
  and music director)
Melvin Jackson, saxophone and MC (bandleader)
Stanley Abernathy, trumpet—formerly with Bobby "Blue" Bland, Gladys
  Knight, The Dells and The Manhattans
James "Boogaloo" Bolden, trumpet—formerly with Duke Ellington's
  Orchestra (B.B.'s band leader for twenty-plus years)

The concert was scheduled to start at seven in the evening, but an hour passed before the band made their way to the stage. While the audience got situated with items from the concession area in the lobby, a DJ in the side balcony nook turned out oldies but goodies. The music piped through the theater and threaded its way into the feet and shoulders of the listeners. Folks sang, swayed and kept up with the beat of the masterful DJ's selections. You could tell that he was a cool cat from way back, but his middle age paunch gave away the fact that he was somebody's grandfather. He was no longer a cool cat but still a cat who had a knack for picking out some fine tunes.

When the King's Men made their way onto the stage, the crowd roared. These were older gentlemen, and they were immaculately dressed. B.B. King almost always wore a suit. His cousin had once told him that he would stand a head taller than some of the other musicians if he dressed the part, and it became part of who he was as a musician. It was the trademark of his band's

Crowd lining up in front of the Warfield Theatre in San Francisco. *Courtesy of Diane Williams.*

B.B. King performing
in Fort Yates, North
Dakota, on November
10, 2001. *Courtesy of
Billy Johnson.*

commitment to professionalism. One of the few times they changed their attire from wearing suits was when King came home to perform in Indianola. It wasn't unusual to see them all wearing Hawaiian shirts.

The synchronized horn blast carried an energy guaranteed to chase the blues away. The drummer fleshed out beats that made you want to scream. The beats were delivered in rapid-fire succession, hand over arm, wrists twisting with possibilities. The bass player held the beats religiously while standing in a relaxed manner, never grandstanding his talents. In fact, the band's delivery was carried out in such a way that every note resonated with harmony.

The King's Men showed off their talents by taking turns as lead, while the other musicians faded slightly into the background. They played tunes like "Manhattan Blues." They were warming up the crowd, loosening up the people sitting in the theater chairs and preparing for some of the King's signature-style playing and singing. Interestingly, King would never play and sing at the same time.

After approximately thirty minutes, B.B. King finally took the stage. The crowd had patiently waited for this gentleman to do what he did best: play Lucille like the master he was. King was known to attack the guitar through lead work and quick fills, then he would sing a bit while the guitar hung across his chest, waiting for its turn to solo. Unlike other professional guitarists, he didn't chord between solos or while singing, but he would take turns playing guitar and then singing masterfully throughout the concert.

The King was eighty-eight years old, and this concert suggested that his touring days were winding down. Yet when King started to sing, his fans could attest to the fact that his voice still had a hint of that special something.

This page: B.B. King at the Jackson R & B Festival. *Courtesy of Amile Wilson.*

There was evidence that it was fading, but it was still strong. The musicality in his guitar playing took everyone by surprise. The signature trills were gone, but it didn't matter. B.B. King was loved. His fans would never betray that love. He talked, the band played, he sang, the band played and every now and then he played the guitar before finally giving it back to the band to "show their stuff."

Never satisfied, King spent his entire life trying to achieve the next level of musicality. It was always there just beyond his fingertips. At times, it gave him some anxiety because it was his dream to accomplish more with music. He spent his life chasing that dream. There are musicians who perform and know that they have accomplished their lifelong dreams, and there are musicians who have achieved levels of success, thinking they were the greatest, though they may have just been riding momentary waves of success. B.B. King never settled for anything less than putting his heart, soul and creativity into his music. It was his hope to surpass each performance with the goal of bringing a deeper awareness to the music called blues. And on that night at the Warfield Theatre in San Francisco, after nearly nine decades of life, he did it again.

PART I

The Life and Legacy of B.B. King

HUMBLE BEGINNINGS

He is sincere, honest, true, for real, and genuine.
—*Carlos Santana*

R iley B. King was born on September 16, 1925. His birth was not formally documented, which was often the case for African Americans during and prior to that time. It is said that he was named after the plantation owner of the land on which he was born, a white man named Jim O'Reilly. His parents dropped the "O" because they said that Riley "didn't look Irish." Some written accounts reference his father's long-lost brother as having the same name. The family talk was that Riley's uncle disappeared many years earlier—before King was born—and that he was never seen again. Interestingly, Riley's middle initial was not defined during the earlier days of his life but would take on meaning when he began to branch out as a musician in Memphis, Tennessee.

Riley was born on a Wednesday in a small cabin along the banks of Bear Creek. The cabin was crude—you could look through the cracks in the wood and determine the time of day. The house had neither electricity nor indoor plumbing, and the family had to use buckets to keep water from splashing on the floor when it rained.

The town in which he was born is known as Berclair, Mississippi. It is an unincorporated community in Leflore County and is three miles west of Itta Bena. Riley's birth is also referenced as having taken place along the banks of Blue Lake. These are all legitimate references of nearby landmarks, and

B.B. King and the band at Club Ebony. *Courtesy of Ralph Smith.*

it is not unfounded that King would also call nearby Indianola home. People in rural communities would often call a nearby place their home of origin. In Mississippi and in many Southern communities, people staked claim to references that added validity to their places of origin because those areas were either more populated, where they spent much of their time or were points along the path of industry and resources, thus were more recognizable.

Riley's parents were Albert and Nora Ella King. They had another child named Curce King, who was three years younger than Riley. He lived two years and died from eating broken glass. Riley was deeply saddened by his brother's death.

Life was hard for the King family. They lived in the Mississippi Delta, and only two years after Riley was born, the Great Mississippi River Flood of 1927 took place. In one of the most devastating floods in America's history, more than twenty-seven thousand square miles were covered in water that reached up to thirty feet high. Many African Americans who lived along the lower river were displaced and migrated north to cities such as Chicago, Detroit and Milwaukee. The waters started with extremely heavy rainfalls during the summer of 1926 and continued with the swelling of tributaries in surrounding states. Southerners fought back by building levees, but the force of water was overwhelming and broke through the levees. Loss of

THE LIFE AND LEGACY OF B.B. KING

agriculture, livestock, human lives and livelihood were great, and those who remained were displaced for months. The disparity that took place in nearby Greenville in rescuing whites and blacks from the area is well documented but rarely mentioned. As whites were rescued, many African Americans were left to their own devices for survival. Most were manual laborers, and many were enlisted to help build the levees. Some were smart enough to remove themselves from the area, but the King family remained in the Delta.

This was not the only test of this family's fortitude. Albert and Nora were young, and their life as sharecroppers was extremely difficult and created a stressful home environment. Even the children had to work as child labor was an acceptable activity prior to World War II. In those days, learning and education took place at the feet of parents either in the home or while chores were being done. For African Americans in the South, emphasis was placed less on education and more on cotton picking season and the time of year for planting and harvesting crops.

Riley King and his father did not have a traditional father-son relationship. Albert never told the boy he loved him, and Riley was left to wonder if his father even cared for him. In fact, his father never even called him by his first name. He sometimes called his son Jack, a name that had no point of reference. He even called him B.B., but that was short for Baby Brother. Riley was eventually separated from his father when his mother left their home and moved to the hills east of the Mississippi Delta, where they lived near Nora's extended family. This was before Riley was hardly school age.

King then lived with his mother and her new husband, Elger Baskin, also known as Picaninee. Nora married a third time, though she was sickly. She had big spots of blood clots in her eyes. She went blind and wasted away due to complications from diabetes. She passed away in 1935 when she was only thirty-one and Riley was just nine years old. He said that losing his mother was "worse than a man coming in a hoodie with a sickle" to take his mother away. His mother's death left him grieving and devastated. He lived with his grandmother, Elnora Farr, for a year, then he lived on his own for a short time, and then with aunts and uncles in the Montgomery County community of Kilmichael, Mississippi, after his grandmother's death.

King remembered visiting his Aunt Jemima (Aunt Mima). She would always kiss him. It was an act that should have represented the love he so desperately needed, but instead he dreaded those visits. Aunt Mima would kiss him as if it were the most natural thing in the world, and it wouldn't have been a problem if she didn't indulge in the habit of dipping snuff. She would

B.B. King performing at homecoming 2011. *Courtesy of Ken Flynt.*

pinch a wad of tobacco out of a tin, pack it into her mouth and hold the big lump on one side of her jaw.

Aunt Mima's home was also the place where Riley had an opportunity to discover music because his aunt had an old Victrola record player. He would listen to her albums, and that was where he heard such musicians as Blind Lemon Jefferson and Lonnie Johnson. They were early influences, and he began to absorb the rhythms and patterns of the blues.

2

EDUCATION FROM THE COTTON FIELDS TO THE SCHOOLHOUSE TO THE CHURCH HOUSE

I'm the country boy that left the country, but they never got the country out of me.
—*B.B. King, NPR Music Interview*

Riley King didn't receive very much education. As a child laborer, it was uncommon to be afforded an opportunity to leave the cotton fields for school, but when he did go to school, he would walk at least five miles to Elkhorn. He attended the Elkhorn School, which was maintained by the Elkhorn Primitive Baptist Church. The school was located across the road from the church. He fondly remembers one of his teachers, Luther H. Henson, not only teaching him basic subjects but also about progressive African Americans, such as Booker T. Washington, Mary McLeod Bethune and Frederick Douglass. Henson also taught him strategies for life because in those days, African American teachers sometimes went beyond the call of duty. Of course, they taught basic subjects such as math, science, writing and reading, but they also took on the task of helping guide students through life by teaching manners, character, cleanliness and general hygiene. They would supply students with soap, toothpaste and other necessities, often taking part of their meager salaries to do so. Henson encouraged such things as abstinence from smoking and drinking. He would say, "You have one house—your body." Riley learned life principles like self-reliance and fair-mindedness, as well as skills that would help him assess his life and make improvements as needed. Henson helped Riley through a rite of passage from childhood to young adulthood by teaching him the ethics of what it meant to work hard, to have tenacity and to have faith—skills every young person needed to grow into becoming a man or woman.

Henson's grave at Elkhorn Primitive Baptist Church Cemetery in Kilmichael, Montgomery County, Mississippi, reads:

Father—Teacher
With a vision for his people
Luther H. (Herron) Henson
1899–2001 (101)
22nd of 23 children

Luther H. Henson's obituary is a testimony to his life and legacy. It appeared in the *Winona Times* on March 15, 2001, and stated, "While a teacher, Mr. Henson managed to give the young people a positive self-image, got them hooked on the idea of self-improvement and gave them an optimistic idea of their prospects in life."

Most of the time, black children were not able to go to school because they started working as regular farm hands as young as seven years old. It is said that field hands worked from "can [pronounced "kin"] to can't." King described it as working "from when you can see to when you cannot see." He remembered workers traveling with a mule across the field and said, "If you did that six days a week, six months out of the year, up to thirty miles a day, for eighteen years, it would be equivalent to traveling around the world."

Even though children had to work in the fields as laborers, they were still children. Young King would often be found playing quietly in the middle of the night until twelve or one in the morning. Riley didn't grow up watching television, but he did get the opportunity to experience ten-cent vendors, or soundies, when he went to Indianola. Soundies were short films from the 1940s that included song, dance and band or orchestra music in regular formulas and are remembered today for clips such as "Our Gang," the comedians Smith and Dale and "Keystone Cops." For the young people of Riley's era, these films were engaging because black children would often get to see someone on the screen who looked like them. This gave them the opportunity to dream of possibilities. The performers included Duke Ellington, Fats Waller (Thomas Wright), Dorothy Dandridge, Billy Eckstine, Count Basie, the Mills Brothers, Sarah Vaughan, Cab Calloway, Lena Horne, Louis Armstrong, Nat King Cole, Jackie "Moms" Mabley and Stepin Fetchit, among many others.

It was an exciting time for dreamers. The performers of that era spoke well, dressed well and lived out their dreams without regard for stereotypical racial barriers. They were the pioneers ushering in the next era of opportunity for blacks. Their dreams and their cultural pride overshadowed the racial disparities they faced each day.

Grandfathers to soundies were music boxes and player pianos. These used either paper rolls, metal disks or metal cylinders to play musical selections. Next came the coin-operated jukeboxes and phonographs of the 1890s. Soundies, which were prevalent from 1940 to 1946, preceded the era when television was widely accessible. Ten cents was a lot of money when Riley was growing up—a youngster really had to save to be able to afford to put a dime into one of the Panoram machines to see a three-minute soundie. The system had an eighteen-by-twenty-two-inch screen and housed a sixteen-millimeter projector. Soundies used optical soundtracks encoded onto the film, and the film moved along the optical reader. The machines held eight selections that had to be viewed in numerical order. If you started with number four, you would have to look at five, six and seven before you could view eight because the selections were on a continual loop, and the viewer had to place a coin in to see and hear each one. Soundies left an impression on young Riley because the African American performers of his day were classy, stylish and revered.

The blues songs of those days were sung by such minstrel and vaudeville singers as Gertrude "Ma" Rainey, Bessie Smith and Louis Armstrong. The journey of black music is multi-faceted, and in his early encounters with music, King watched it expand in scope from spirituals, ragtime and Delta blues, to boogie-woogie, swing jazz and urban blues. Music progressed from the survival songs of slaves in the cotton fields to an entirely different tempo during Reconstruction, and by the Jim Crow era, it began to reflect the diverse aspects of life beyond field labor.

That said, when King was a little boy, parents did not allow their children to sing the folk songs that the minstrel and vaudeville singers brought to waterfront communities. This was superstitiously called "devil's music" because of its blatant lack of calling on God for strength and sustenance and because it seemed to memorialize the struggles of the times. Many children experienced whippings with the vines from bushes when they were overheard singing the blues. Therefore, Riley grew to love the singing of spirituals and jubilee songs of the era.

Riley's mother was a devout woman. She taught him morals and a belief that the ultimate goodness of all God's creatures was the foundation of one's outlook, and she taught him that faith in God was the standard journey of a Christian's life. While attending Elkhorn Primitive Baptist Church in Kilmichael, King joined the church choir at a very young age. He joined a gospel singing group with his cousin Birkett Davis and their friends Walter Doris Jr. and Dubois Hane. They named themselves the Jubilee Singers and tried to sound like a group called the Golden Gate Quartet, but a good try was all they could accomplish.

Singing in the choir gave King an opportunity to look out at the congregation and notice the goings-on. One thing that stood out to him was his pastor, the Reverend Archie Fair. Fair played electric guitar, and Riley was enamored with the way he handled the instrument. The Reverend Fair's wife and King's uncle William Pullian's wife were sisters. During a visit in one of their homes, the two sisters allowed Riley to touch the reverend's guitar. It was a magical moment. After that, he couldn't control his thoughts. He wanted one of the instruments for himself. The way the reverend played made Riley's imagination soar. Although the Baptists prohibited guitar playing in the church and discouraged the playing of the instrument outside of the church during the early twentieth century, the Pentecostal and Holiness congregations welcomed it, along with the playing of the drums and tambourine.

At the age of twelve, King was working on the plantation of Flake and Zelma Cartledge. He purchased his first guitar with a fifteen-dollar advance that Mr. Cartledge gave him. The money did not go to waste, and he immediately began learning how to play. King learned to play the E, A and B chords by watching the way Reverend Fair handled the guitar. Fair projected a charismatic influence that brought church members together in high praise and worship. Every Sunday, Fair presented a soulful musical event.

It was common practice that members were known by their first names during the week and as Brother or Sister on Sunday. You were somebody on Sunday at Reverend Archie Fair's church. This was a tradition that went on in many churches across America, but it was especially endearing to the African Americans who labored in the fields every day and who were treated as if they were less than whites in the community. The church was a place where they could dress up in their best clothes on Sunday and wear their dignity and respect with their heads held high.

In collaboration with the music of the day, the Mississippi Delta spiritual singing included hand clapping and foot drumming in a rhythmic stepping pattern. At the time, Dr. Isaac Watts's songs were commonly sung

Young B.B. King from the Martha King Family Collection. *Courtesy of Mary Alice Smith.*

throughout the South. The Dr. Watts style of singing was created out of necessity by African Americans in the Mississippi Delta because the churches often didn't have hymnals and many people were unable to read even if there were hymnals. Dr. Watts's style was a hymn-singing tradition that is called "lining-out," which is a tradition that originated in Africa and was passed down to people of African descent. It is commonly known as call and response. One person would pitch the song for the congregation, then the congregation would line-out what the person pitching the words had just sung by using the same melody and rhythm in repeat. They would hold on to the melody using vocal embellishments and moans for a longer time than had originally been pitched. Over time, guitar and piano playing slowly began to replace shape-note singing and the Dr. Watts style of call-and-response singing in churches. These types of musical renderings that came from Reverend Fair's guitar playing left a mark on Riley King.

Riley King's grandmother, Elnora Farr, died after a brief illness in January 1940. King continued to live in her cabin and farmed and raised cotton on Edwayne Henderson's farm. At the time of her death, Riley's grandmother was still in debt to Henderson, and the cabin didn't have electricity. The boy was lonely. This experience left him with an uneasy feeling. He remained uncomfortable in dark rooms for his entire life and always kept a flashlight nearby.

About this time in his life, he said,

> *I swore as a poor kid that when I grew up I would have what I wanted to eat when I wanted to eat it and I would never sleep in a dark room. For a little boy sleeping alone in the Delta, the nights were very, very dark. After my mama died, I stayed with some of my relatives for a while, and they would talk about ghosts and then at nine o'clock say, "It's time to go to bed, boy." And then they'd cut the lantern. So, I do not sleep in a dark room even if there's somebody with me.*

His grandmother's situation was not uncommon. Sharecroppers were often unable to fully repay plantation owners. It was a form of oppression because sharecroppers worked for wages and in turn had to pay the landowner for supplies, food, clothing and other incidentals. At the time of Farr's death, her debt totaled $21.75, which at the time was a lot of money. It was equivalent to more than five months of wages.

Henderson allowed Riley to stay in Elnora Farr's cabin alone while working for him. Even though he only made $2.50 as a monthly allowance, King did his best to repay his grandmother's debt and left a balance of $7.54, which was eventually settled by a government subsidy. After a year, King's father went to get him and moved the young man in with his new family in Lexington, Mississippi. He only stayed with his father for two years. They were never close, and his father had another son and three daughters to consider. Riley just didn't feel like he fit in with his half-siblings. He longed to be back in Kilmichael, going to the Elkhorn School and singing with the gospel group. One day, he got on his bicycle and rode approximately fifty miles back to Kilmichael.

In 1943, Riley moved to Indianola and worked on Johnson Barrett's plantation. His job was to drive the tractor and sharecrop, and he was paid one dollar a day for his work. During this time, he started another gospel group with his cousin Birkett Davis and a guy by the name of John Matthews. They formed a five-man ensemble called the St. John's Gospel Singers, and Riley was the guitar player. The group found work on the radio station WGRM in Greenwood, and there would often be a packed church house of listeners whenever they performed. Audiences loved them. They eventually became known as the Famous St. John's Gospel Singers.

King was eligible for the draft in this same year, but the owner of the plantation where he worked encouraged him to get married and helped him secure an occupational deferment from the war. He spent some time in a military training camp but received the postponement because he was a valuable tractor driver, and the army reclassified him as being needed on the farm.

In time, the blues started to overshadow the gospel music that he played. When King wasn't singing with the group, he played on a street corner, and folks would give him money. That appealed to King. In those days, it was considered a sin to sing spirituals or gospel music *and* blues music, and it was considered a sin to hang out in juke joints. The Queen of Gospel Music, Mahalia Jackson, was known to say that "any Negro can sing the blues." She wanted to be known for giving God glory through Christian song. Someone had to "pull his [Riley's] coattail" and tell him that he couldn't sing in the quartet and sing the blues. He had to make a choice!

But King loved blues music and knew that he had to spread the word. Gospel music gained him a following and a compliment, but it didn't garner the kind of money that he was paid when he played the blues. The members of the gospel group were satisfied, but King wanted to be a professional musician. He wanted to rise above the cotton fields of the Mississippi Delta, and performing the blues was a much more lucrative opportunity at the time.

Talented and good looking, he was known to catch a young girl's eye. He met Martha Denton, and after a brief courtship, they married on November 27, 1944. (See interview with Mary Alice Smith, chapter nine, for additional information.) The two shared a cabin with Riley's cousin Birkett Davis and his wife, Delicia. Riley and his wife remained together for eight years, but King was young and ambitious.

He was singing with the Famous St. John's Gospel Singers at the time, but he knew that there was a whole world out there and musical opportunities that he wanted to experience. While the group was well known locally and over the radio airwaves, because so many people listened to the radio back then, the group was never actually famous. The Famous St. John's Gospel Singers tried to hold King to the same principles he was taught by his mother, grandmother and the church—namely to acknowledge God in all things along the journey. But when the scales of conscience were weighed in the balance, King made the decision to seek success instead of a nod, a hand clap and foot tap, followed by an affirming amen. His musical talents were blossoming, and it was much more interesting to be known as a blues performer than it was to be known as a gospel singer, especially since his gospel group was not willing to expand on their career beyond their reputation.

In the book *Can't Be Satisfied: The Life and Times of Muddy Waters*, author Robert Gordon wrote, "King played uptown blues, his stinging guitar runs [are] couched in urbanized horn arrangements." He continued by quoting Muddy Waters, "I play cotton-patch music, cornfield, fish fry, B.B. and Albert (King) are a different style, a higher class of people'd see them."

King would travel down to Church Street in Indianola, where many of the townspeople would hang out on the weekends. They walked or hitched a ride into town to be part of the night life. This was where alcohol and gambling nurtured the less desirable bad boy mentality. On Saturdays, children and adults, when they were not working, loved to go to town and

This page and opposite B.B. King at the King Biscuit Blues Festival in October 2010, Helena, Arkansas. *Courtesy of Ken Flynt.*

Unveiling of the B.B. King statue in Indianola. (*Left to right*) B.B. King, Carver Randal and Senator Willie Simmons. *Courtesy of Billy Johnson.*

look around, window shop and people watch. Church Street had a carnival atmosphere, and people came from all around the countryside.

In 1986, B.B. King's footprints, handprints and signature were inlaid on the sidewalk on the east side of Church Street, just south of Second Street in Indianola. King has always said that Indianola was home, and the people there consider him as their own. His 1970 album *Indianola Mississippi Seeds* is a testament to the town.

Before Club Ebony opened in Indianola, the original owner, John Jones, opened Jones Night Spot on Church Street. The Mississippi Blues Trail notes that Riley King would peer through the slats to get a glimpse of performances by such notables as Sonny Boy Williamson II (Rice Miller). Even though Indianola was a small town, the night spot included recognized performers, some of whom had performed nationally.

3

BIGOTRY AND PREJUDICE

It was badder than bad.
—*Reverend (David) Matthews, Bell Grove Baptist Church in Indianola*

T he long-term effects of segregation have historically been expressed through economic depression, reprisals and injustices, as well as discouragements against blacks voting and equal opportunities. Riley King saw his share of prejudice and inequality. The less recognized face of racism was felt in the evil stares, subtle body gestures, vocal intonations, emotional outbursts and demeaning references that attempted to strangle the dignity from a person's spirit.

Stories such as the one about Leon McTatie, who was flogged to death by six white men and lynched in Lexington in July 1945, for allegedly stealing a saddle, were a reminder of the sad realities of race relations in the South. Riley had heard about executions, castrations and lynchings. These were still happening all over the state. A mob of white folks in Lexington castrated a black boy and dragged his body to the courthouse and killed him. King saw it. He never forgot it.

Prior to the civil rights era, there were few folks like plantation owner Johnson Barrett who were civil to those under their employ. What is known or referenced by King and his relationships working with whites was not typical of the Mississippi Delta. In fact, there were white plantation overseers who wore guns and were prepared to use them against blacks. For certain, there were many Ku Klux Klansmen (KKK) who lived in the region.

A Southern idiom stated:

Mule died—buy another one
Kill a nigger—hire another one
That's just the way it was
Yes sir—No Sir
That's just the way it was
Don't talk back—That's just the way it was

The White Citizens' Council, or Citizens Council, was a national organization that was first recognized in Indianola, Mississippi, in July 1954. The council was made of white plantation owners and businessmen from a variety of professional backgrounds, many of whom had great economic influence. Deemed to be a nonviolent group, their operations were clandestine in nature and supportive of the violent activities of the Klan and others. King had already left the area by this time, but he looked back on Mississippi and the South and felt deep sadness.

The White Citizens' Council was a response to the decision in *Brown v. Board of Education* to end segregation. Its efforts to hinder equal opportunity for blacks were succeeding. When Dr. Martin Luther King and others were attacked during the bus boycott in Montgomery, Dr. King spoke out. At that same time, the council doubled in membership. In one of Dr. King's speeches in New York in 1956, he described the council as a modern-day Klan.

He said:

They must be held responsible for all of the terror, the mob rule, and brutal murders that have encompassed the south over the last several years. It is an indictment on America and democracy that these ungodly and unethical and un-Christian and un-American councils have been able to exist…without a modicum of criticism from the federal government.

Dr. King lived long enough to see their power fade.

Sometimes King and his band would travel eighteen hours at a time. Those were especially hard, turbulent times for black musicians who were forced to go without many of the conveniences that should have been afforded to everyone. Black musicians during the late nineteenth and early twentieth centuries feared attacks from the Ku Klux Klan and would often go out of their way—off the main roadways, traveling longer distances—to get to their destinations. They could not eat in the same restaurants, drink from the same water fountains or receive the same wages for a day's work. There were cases where they couldn't even enter from the same door and were often required to enter from a door in the rear of a building. The racism, bigotry and hatred created a climate that was perplexing to Riley King. He wished for the times to be better, but he never let those dark days turn him against humanity.

Riley experienced what many blacks in the South experienced: blatant prejudice and horrid inconveniences. Jim Crow laws (1877–1954) reinforced racial segregation. They determined that blacks were not allowed to drink from public water fountains that were designated for whites or use "whites only" restrooms, and in some instances, blacks were not allowed to walk along the same sidewalk as whites. Blacks could not stay in the same hotels, which was hard on the health of black musicians traveling between performances. Traveling along back roads, they were not allowed to eat at the same lunch counters and tables as others. Because of this so-called backdoor policy, blacks might not get to eat and would have to travel with their own nonperishable food items, such as Vienna sausages, canned goods, crackers and sandwiches. This led to poor eating habits, high blood pressure, heart trouble and diabetes. Sometimes entertainers would resort to taking drugs, which also debilitated their health. The legal system offered no assistance for these inequalities, and there were very few blacks working in the legal system as policemen, city officials or lawyers. Even when blacks were in those positions, there was not much they could do. Their hands were tied because those attitudes were prevalent and woven throughout all of society, including government.

The Jim Crow era was a time in the United States' history when efforts were made to keep blacks and whites separated by instituting laws that diminished the rights and privileges of blacks. The era started in the southern states after the Civil War. The term was adopted from a minstrel show characterization (white person in blackface makeup) in which someone sang the song "Jump Jim Crow." The name became the mantra for inequality. There was also a dance called Jump Jim Crow that was attributed to white minstrel performer Thomas Dartmouth "Daddy" Rice in 1828.

On the road, King and his musicians had to search for hotels that would allow black patrons, and musicians often had to stay in rooming houses. King's bus was his rolling house, but the road was not very glamorous when segregation was at its height. King learned to let gas station attendants put fuel in the tank while asking about the restrooms. If he was told the restrooms were out of order, he would tell the attendant to stop pumping the gas. Using restrooms, drinking from water fountains and eating in restaurant areas designated for whites could lead to a black person losing their life. It was a very inconvenient time for blacks.

In December 1998, one of King's anecdotes was related in a *Rolling Stones* article by Gerri Hirshey titled "On the Bus with B.B. King." Hirshey summarized the story:

> *He's trudging down a dusty two-lane, a lone, worried black man in too-fine clothes. Dawn is breaking as he comes to a whites-only cafe and walks around, instinctively, to the back door. The owner is just opening up when B.B. identifies himself and explains his problem: a breakdown, a busload of hungry musicians. Sure would help if they could come in and sit down. The man says OK and sets up a table. As the band wolfs biscuits and gravy, the jumpy owner stands at the front door, greeting his white regulars. To each he blurts apologetically: "That's B.B. King and his band. The bus broke down and…"*

Hirshey went on to say King laughed at the vision of the nervous but kindly man who dared serve him a square meal beneath the menacing wings of Jim Crow. "I'm glad that's changed," King said. "Thank God for the change."

4

SWITCHING GEARS

A consummate gentleman.
—*Eric Clapton referencing B.B. King*

O ne afternoon in the spring of 1947, after working all day in the field for Johnson Barrett, Riley King prepared to return Barrett's tractor to its place near the barn. On this day, a turn of events changed his life forever. While attempting to place the tractor in the neutral gear position, and just before cutting off the engine, King jumped out while the tractor was still in gear. He was anxious to be done with the day's work and ready to hang out in town for an evening and was being a little absentminded, or maybe he was just tired, that afternoon. The tractor backfired and ran smack-dab into the storage shed. It damaged the exhaust pipe when it hit the edge of the overhanging roof. King couldn't imagine facing Barrett. How would he ever pay for the damage? It was unfathomable. He took just enough time to collect his thoughts and grab his guitar. With $2.50 in his pocket, all the money he had to his name, he headed away from town.

He left his livelihood and his wife, caught a grocery company truck and went to Memphis. He landed on Beale Street and found his mother's cousin, Booker T. "Bukka" White. White was a famous blues singer and recording artist, and he became an important influence and mentor to King. King got a job working in a factory with his cousin, but his most memorable times with White were spent listening to and watching him play guitar. The blues that White played represented a style much different

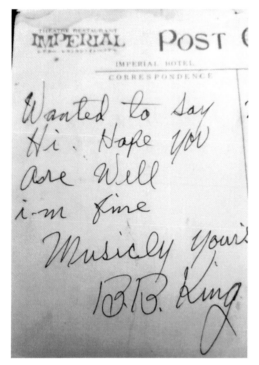

Left: Note to Martha King from B.B. King. From the Martha King Family Collection. *Courtesy of Mary Alice Smith.*

Below: Letter to Martha King. From the Martha King Family Collection. *Courtesy of Mary Alice Smith.*

7-22-2002

MS, MARTHA DAVIDSON
I am thinking of you, but you are thought of" often," I am doing ok, still working a lot, but I am starting to cut back some now, I sent this letter, a year ago, and it came back, I had heard that You had been ill, please lets stay in touch, I guess this is all for now, all the best to You, please stay well,
SINCENELY YOURS
RILEY/B. KING

from the style that Reverend Archie Fair played. As much as King tried, he was never able to achieve the technique that his cousin effortlessly exhibited on the guitar.

All in all, Riley matured into a man of integrity, and his conscience did not allow him to run away from the debt he owed Johnson Barrett. He

Left: Young B.B. King and Martha King. From the Martha King Family Collection. *Courtesy of Mary Alice Smith.*

Right: Martha King. From the Martha King Family Collection. *Courtesy of Mary Alice Smith.*

took his meager earnings and returned to Indianola to work for Johnson Barrett so he could pay his $500–$600 debt. Thankfully, Johnson Barrett was known to be an agreeable man, and he let King come back to work on the farm. King made approximately fifteen dollars a day driving a farm tractor on the Barrett plantation, but he was determined to pay his debt, and he did.

5

BEALE STREET

I didn't think of Memphis as Memphis. I thought of Beale Street as Memphis.
—*B.B. King*

When King returned to Memphis looking for Bukka White in 1948, he had no idea where to find him. But just asking around town in those days could lead to someone pointing a person in the direction they needed to look. Bukka was a musician, so he wasn't hard to find.

King stayed with his cousin for ten months, and there was a lot going on in those ten months. It was a memorable time for dance shows, Rabbit Foot Minstrel performances, amateur shows and much more. It was a smorgasbord of entertainment. Memphis was more famous than New Orleans at that time, and Bukka tried to teach King what he knew about playing the guitar. White played slide guitar in an open-tuning style. King was never able to capture White's style of using the metal cylinder to slide across the guitar, nor was he able to mimic White's fingering style. It was fancy stuff for a novice like King, but by the late '40s, White's acoustic country blues approach was out of style. White was only able to teach King the basics, such as the proper way to hold a guitar and how to phrase his lyrics. On his own, King learned how to trill the guitar strings to make the sound of the steel cylinder that Bukka wore on his finger to slide across the neck of the guitar.

"LUES BOY" KING

EXCLUSIVE RECORDING ARTIST
EXCLUSIVE BUFFALO BOOKING ARTIST
2307 Erastus Street
Houston, Texas
ORchard 786

B.B. King. From
Martha King's
Family Collection.
*Courtesy of Mary
Alice Smith.*

In *African Folklore: An Encyclopedia*, editors Philip M. Peek and Kwesi Yankah referenced a comparison of the stringed instruments of Africa to African American musicians:

> *African American musicians utilize comparatively short, rhythmic, melodic building blocks, typical of the savannah region of Africa. These short, rhythmic, melodic phrases, or riffs, were enhanced by various African techniques such as bending notes, hammering on, pulling off, damping the strings for rhythmic effect, or hitting on the body of the instruments.*

What King remembered most was that White taught him that whenever he performed, he should act and dress professionally. He told him, "Dress like you're going to the bank for money." Bukka also taught King about life as a musician—how to be resilient in the industry because it could break a man down. Playing long hours, often in juke joints and smoky party houses, took its toll on many musicians. The nightlife, fast women and dangerous and shady goings-on could end a musician's career at an early age.

Booker T. Washington "Bukka" White recorded a pair of religious songs in 1930: "I Am in the Heavenly Way" and "Promise True and Grand." His hit song was "Shake 'Em on Down." White was indicted for shooting a man and convicted in Aberdeen and sent to Parchman Farm Prison (Mississippi State Penitentiary) from 1937 to 1940. He was released through a governor's pardon, according to researcher Gayle Dean Wardlow. The pardon was likely related to his status as a recording artist. White recorded *Parchman Farm Blues* for John Lomax, a teacher and musicologist, and Alan Lomax, an ethnomusicologist, archivist, field advisor, writer and filmmaker.

Another musician from the time who let the industry get to him was Robert Johnson (1911–1938). For decades, people have debated whether this guitar player, famous for his mastery of the instrument, sold his soul to the devil at the crossroads of Highways 49 and 61 in the Mississippi Delta. It is a great myth and a good story that continues to be told. Johnson was an itinerant musician who walked around from place to place with his guitar strapped on his back. He was always looking for opportunity. Before he made it to the crossroads, he was known to be a good harmonica player but a bad guitar player. Practice and more practice will help a person become better at something, but Johnson was young. It seemed that he learned and developed rapidly and became a prolific musician in a very short period of time. Folks just didn't believe that someone could accomplish as much as Johnson did so quickly. Hardly anyone gave him credit for putting in the hard work.

According to Bruce Conforth, there is a more practical account that explains how Johnson learned to play so well. It seems that Isaiah "Ike" Zimmerman, who lived in Beauregard, Mississippi, taught Johnson to play around 1931. Ike was known to perform in juke joints, but he also had a gift for teaching. Johnson was traveling around the area of Martinsville and Hazlehurst when he met Zimmerman. He traveled back to Beauregard with Zimmerman and ended up spending some time learning and practicing with him in the Beauregard Cemetery. Like many upcoming musicians who were looking for a way out of the cotton fields, Johnson's desire to be a great musician superseded rational thinking. To his own detriment and demise, he made a few bad decisions in his young life. At least that's what folks were saying. At the age of twenty-seven, it is said that he was poisoned for trying to steal another man's woman, and it is alleged that the devil gave him three extra days to live while the poison was still running through his veins.

Mississippi Devil's Crossroad— old US Highway 61 and old US Highway 49. Clarksdale, Mississippi. *Courtesy of Susan Liles.*

During King's early days as a musician, men gravitated to the Home of the Blues: Memphis. They would gather on Beale Street and perform, hoping someone would be inspired to put a coin in a tip jar or hat that was placed strategically on the ground. Memphis is also the place where musicians learned from one another. They would willingly share or brag about their unique styles. Original techniques and instrumental manipulations arose from endless hours of practice and a strong taste for success.

Desiring to be a recognized musician, King had an even greater interest in sharing what this music meant to him and what it should have meant to the world. This took him into beer halls, juke joints and nightclubs where he played to the feverish pitch of hip swaying, handclapping and sashaying. Those night spots featured music, dancing and gambling.

It is said that the word *juke* is derived from the Gullah word *joog*, which means to be disorderly or rowdy. In Zora Neale Hurston's essay "Characteristics of Negro Expression," published in 1934, she wrote:

> *"Jook" is a word for a Negro pleasure house. It may mean a bawdy house. It may mean the house set apart on public works where the men and women dance, drink and gamble. Often, it is a combination of these….They may have acquired their flavor from an association with the work camp culture in the South. It served as a resort night spot where laborers, such as turpentine workers, could take their evening relaxation deep in the pine forests.*

Juke joints were considered recreational entertainment. They were social releases of sorts, away from the "give-a-cares" of society. When King later started performing on the road, he was willing to pay his dues for the opportunity to play the blues, so he performed in beer halls and along the Chitlin' Circuit, learning a lot from other performers, such as the Rabbit Foot Minstrels.

The Chitlin' Circuit was the name given to entertainment venues throughout the South and Midwest where black musicians and a variety of other entertainers performed. These were opportunities for talented blacks who might not otherwise have a venue to hone their skills. These were also places where men and women could relax and let their hair down. They could congregate, dance and release the last ounce of energy from a tough work week or just forget their worries.

King would often sleep in the back rooms of beer halls and play on the streets for tips while trying to stay focused on becoming recognized as a blues musician. At the age of twenty-three, he learned to discipline himself and never lost sight of his dream. By the late 1940s, his hard work began to pay off, and around 1950, he was starting to make a name for himself. He knew that if he gave up on his dream, he would not be able to enjoy even such basic necessities as eating. Sharecropping was too hard of a life, and it was not something one would want to settle on as a career to sustain a man and his family. King knew that he had something worthy of his efforts. He believed in himself.

Early on, young Riley King studied and explored the music of Blind Boy Fuller, Blind Lemon Jefferson and T-Bone Walker. He didn't try to play like them, but he learned from them and came away with his own musical expression. He acknowledged how great they were and recognized that no one else was playing like them at the time. They were the first. They were the pioneers. This music became popular, but some African American preachers were not well educated, and they didn't understand how to put life and religion together. They didn't know how to make the connection, so they remained as close to the Bible as possible.

King had a signature style and a soulful voice, and Memphis was the Mecca for good musicians, but many of them played their instruments and sang much better than King. It was on Beale Street that he realized he was nothing special. There were hundreds of others like him. He never got over that feeling and believed there was always more that he could learn and achieve with his musicality. He spent his life trying to achieve it. His personal style did not come from the Mississippi Delta Blues. He listened to 78 records and heard blues from outside the region. He was heavily influenced by Kansas City big band jazz, most notably Count Basie.

While living in Indianola, King would listen to Sonny Boy Williamson II on the radio. Williamson began as the host of King Biscuit Time (KBT) in 1941, around the time the station was established. KBT is the longest-running daily radio show in history and can still be heard in Indianola, Mississippi. The show was sponsored and named after locally distributed King Biscuit Flour. It was over KFFA radio station in Helena, Arkansas, that

King first heard Williamson and Robert Jr. Lockwood performing. In 1948, King went to KWEM radio station in West Memphis, Arkansas, which was located just across the river from Memphis, Tennessee.

Williamson was a debonair blues artist and a legend on blues harp who earned credits and awards in his own right. There was another musician who went by the name of Sonny Boy Williamson. It was not uncommon in those days for an up-and-coming artist to take the name of another well-known artist. Williamson II wasn't recognized as a legend until after his demise. Other musicians who are known to have presented in the early days on the show were Pinetop Perkins and James "Peck" Curtis. They were part of the original band called the King Biscuit Entertainers. This was the first radio station to feature blues.

Williamson helped King land a gig at the Sixteenth Street Grill in West Memphis. A female juke joint owner promised that if he could get a spot on the radio station like that of Sonny Boy Williamson, she would hire him more often to play in her juke joint. A spot on the radio station WDIA in Memphis, Tennessee, which had a black audience, paid twelve dollars. Bob Pepper and Bert Ferguson started the station in 1947, and the music started out as a mix of country/western, light pop and blues.

Beale Street was a lively place to hang around. One of the main events was amateur night, which was a talent show for up-and-coming artists. A man by the name of Rufus Thomas (1917–2001) was the emcee. Thomas hosted the show for eleven years. King wanted to play and hoped that Thomas would give him a chance. Everyone had one chance to try out, but Riley played a trick on Thomas. He'd take a turn trying out one night and then the next night he would appear as a band member with Bobby "Blue" Bland. At one time, everyone who played was paid two or three dollars, but the pay went down to one dollar. King showed up every night.

Thomas, who started performing as a little boy, is perhaps best remembered for singing a song called "Walking the Dog" (1965). His career as a singer spanned most of his life as a child and on into adulthood. He has been recognized by the Grammy Hall of Fame for being a rhythm and blues pioneer.

Once King's voice made it to the airwaves on WDIA, his career took off. King's show was called *King's Spot*, and when King was given more airtime, the show became known as the *Sepia Swing Club*. The radio allowed him to let people know when he would be performing on Beale Street.

It was evident that calling King by his given name, Riley, needed to change along with his success. He became known as the Beale Street Blues

Boy, which was later shortened to Blues Boy King. As providence would have it, he took on the most famous initials in all the world, B.B., and his fans loved it. In 1948, things turned around and the station began to appeal to black listeners, a previously untapped market. The station hired musicians early in their careers. When the station increased its power some years later, it could be heard as far away as the Mississippi Gulf Coast, and the idea to reach black audiences spread like a virus around the country. An audition on WDIA landed King a fifteen-minute spot where he first became famous as the Pepticon Boy. King was asked to endorse the tonic, and he is remembered for writing and singing a song advertising the alcohol-laced health liquid. Anyone who heard the song in the late 1940s will also remember the words and the tune. It was a big deal for King to get the product endorsement, and he took it very seriously. He also made the brand very popular.

Eventually, the station transitioned to black management, and black music was heard on the airwaves as far away as New Orleans. King also grew in musical stature and became known as one of the six essential modern blues artists whose impacts on the industry are important to us today. The other five greats are Buddy Guy, Howlin' Wolf, John Lee Hooker, Muddy Waters and Willie Dixon. All six are known the world over. But the name and music that stands out above them all is B.B. King.

When King started out, other musicians didn't pay much attention to him. But he was onto something. One thing is sure, Albert King, Little Milton and B.B. King each had distinct styles and energy. Muddy Waters was a great influence, as were Mississippi musicians Howlin' Wolf, Charley Patton and Son House. They were all originals.

King's first song was named for his first wife, Martha, and was called "Miss Martha King." His first single was cut in 1949. He made his first four singles in the studio at WDIA for the Nashville-based Bullet label. Bullet Records was the fastest growing independent record company in the United States at that time.

Don Kern was the station manager of WDIA, and it is alleged that he shared B.B.'s music with Jules and Saul Bihari when they came for a visit. The Bihari brothers were part of the rhythm and blues and rock and roll trend and were the founders of Modern Records in Los Angeles. After their introduction, King recorded with Modern Records for more than a decade.

King's music continued to increase in popularity, and he was playing gigs all around the area. He was given more and more time on the radio, but as a radio personality, he would not play his own music on the air. Soon he met Robert Henry. Henry was a local businessman who owned a pool hall on Beale Street, and he was a representative of the Musicians Union Local 71. He knew a lot of people in the industry and could get King bookings that drew attention. Henry got King and his Beale Street Blues Band gigs in juke joints in Arkansas, Tennessee and Jackson, Mississippi. After the touring dates started filling his calendar, he gave up his job as a disc jockey. Henry booked King up and down the roadways with performances in black theaters and clubs along the Chitlin' Circuit. In fact, King spent the next ten years on the road, and the road became the place he called home.

6

MAKING MUSIC

After months of constantly rolling a stone, it does not gather moss.
—Proverb

By late 1949 into early 1950, King was becoming a household name in Tennessee, Arkansas and Mississippi. His music was starting to receive recognition on the airwaves. According to the Rock and Roll Hall of Fame, King's career really took off in 1951, when he recorded "Three O'Clock Blues." It was a minor hit for Lowell Fulsom, a guitarist from Oklahoma, but it hit the charts in a major way for B.B. King. He recorded it in a creatively improvised space at a YMCA. He also recorded "That Ain't the Way to Do It" around the same time.

The road to success can have a lot of curves and detours, and King's did. While performing at a juke joint in Twist, Arkansas, King almost lost his guitar and his life. The open room where he was performing was cold. A large metal barrel was placed in the middle of the floor, and rags and paper had been placed inside and ignited with kerosene to warm the room. Men and women avoided the barrel and danced around it. At some point, two men whose tempers were in a bad place started fighting over a woman and knocked the barrel over. The building caught fire, and the patrons immediately fled. King, realizing that his guitar was still inside, foolishly ran back to get it. Two men lost their lives that night, and King was almost burned to death. He vowed to never forget what almost happened to him and named the guitar "Lucille," after the woman over whom the two

Left: Diane Williams carrying King's guitars on the day of the funeral, May 30, 2015. *Courtesy of Glynn Fought.*

Below: B.B. King taking the stage. *Courtesy of Ralph Smith.*

men had been fighting. Today, Lucille is known all over the world, and she is referred to as if she were the only one, though King has had many guitars—all named Lucille.

King and his band didn't have to rehearse because King was getting requests to perform almost every day of the year. In the years before the civil rights era, King and his band toured along the Chitlin' Circuit, but traveling from place to place was not a life to be envied, especially during segregation.

In some ways, B.B. King was a man like any other, but in other ways, he was completely different. When he jerked the guitar to his chest and threw back his head with his eyes tightly closed, you knew that he was about to bring something out from deep within his soul. As his fingers fluttered across the neck of the guitar, his dedication and endless hours of work showed his stubbornness and tenacity, and you knew that he would never give up. His vibrato is known around the world, and it is said that it only takes an intro to recognize that you have just heard B.B. King's voice and music. Blues guitarist and singer George "Buddy" Guy once said, "His voice and his sound were like two peas in one hull." But if you asked B.B. King about his musicality, he would tell you that he was "horrible with chords."

In 1950, King had an opportunity to record at Memphis Recording Service, which was operated by Sam Phillips. It shared a building with Sun Records, the first label that recorded Elvis Presley. With Memphis Recording Service, King's music received national distribution. He was signed to Modern Records, and his records came out on their RPM label. After "Three O'Clock Blues" made it onto the Billboard R & B charts in 1952, he signed with Universal Attractions Booking Agency and performed around the country in cities such as Washington, D.C., Baltimore, Chicago and New York. He performed in recognized theater houses such as the Apollo in Harlem, New York. Though he did not always receive commercial success, it was still an amazing opportunity for a young man from the Mississippi Delta. King was about to embark on a whole new world. He began to perform for a broader audience, and his versatility and charisma grew with each experience. He continued to travel the roadways to the rural juke joints and roadhouses, and he gained the allegiance of blues enthusiasts along the eastern seaboard. B.B. King's music took off, and his music was heard on black radio stations throughout the United States.

King was doing a lot of things right. He partnered with Memphis bandleader Bill Harvey and the Buffalo Booking Agency out of Houston, Texas, when he left Universal Attractions. The company had a recognized name, and this was a collaboration that helped launch King's career to the next level. His relationship with Robert Henry ended, and Evelyn Johnson, a black woman, took over his performance career at the Buffalo Booking Agency. Johnson was the company's business manager and booking agent. She was the founder of the Buffalo Booking Agency, and she studied the industry. She was so successful at booking gigs that B.B. King played 342 one-night stands in 1956.

It is also important to note that King's success helped blues music. Indeed, he worked for the recognition of the music more than personal recognition. Traveling almost every day of the year to showcase his God-given talent was a testament to his desire to perpetuate and preserve the art form. He was a trendsetter moving the blues along, always creatively stretching boundaries with new and distinct licks.

Through all of this, King always remembered where the music came from. The songs of native Africans voiced their soul's rhythms across the waters of the Middle Passage to places like the Americas. Those songs made their way onto the cotton fields and were sung in the hot sun and became a testament to the fortitude of brave men and women who were forced into slave labor and held captive against their will. Those songs are also a testament to the downtrodden and hopeless. Those men and women, less fortunate than anyone would ever desire to be, did not sing death dirges in an effort to hold on. They sang songs of hope that became codes and songs of jubilee. Those songs of hope progressed and became reflections on daily life—its whims and its woes. In turn, they became the songs of people rising up out of sad and depressing situations, from the first years of African captivity in America beginning in 1619, to emancipation in 1865.

Frederick Douglass reflected on these songs, stating,

I have often been utterly astonished, since I came to the north, to find persons who could speak of the singing, among slaves, as evidence of their contentment and happiness. It is impossible to conceive of a greater mistake. Slaves sing most when they are most unhappy. The songs of the slave represent the sorrows of his heart; and he is relieved by them, only as an aching heart is relieved by its tears. At least, such is my experience. I have often sung to drown my sorrow, but seldom to express my happiness. Crying for joy, and singing for joy, were alike uncommon to me while in the jaws of slavery. The singing of a man cast away upon a desolate island might be as appropriately considered as evidence of contentment and happiness, as the singing of a slave; the songs of the one and of the other are prompted by the same emotion.

At the turn of the twentieth century, blues songs were more than just the vocalizations of old men reflecting on hard times, love and loss. Blues songs were sung throughout the Jim Crow era (1877–1954), another period when African Americans struggled with institutionalized oppression and racial segregation.

The late BeBe Moore Campbell wrote the book *Your Blues Ain't Like Mine*. It is a story of fiction based in rural Mississippi and mirrors the life of Emmett Till. Life has a way of grabbing us by the throat and shaking us up a bit. Circumstances in life can be tragic and hard, but it is the individual spirit that rises by whatever means necessary and survives. What the blues tell us is that we may look down on the metaphoric river that reflects our circumstances, but we can sing songs that render another perspective and give us a light-hearted mechanism to rise up and strive to find a way out of our circumstances.

In 1952, at the age of twenty-seven, B.B. King divorced his first wife. They did not have any children together. That same year, another one of his songs, "You Know I Love You," reached number one on the R & B charts. Rhythm and blues was a combined genre of music that became recognized around the same time as rock and roll. At the time, young, often white, music enthusiasts were drawn to rock and roll, but it didn't have the same appeal with black audiences. R & B was the music industry's way to draw a black audience, and it captured the hearts of young people across the United States and beyond. Both genres created a wave of listeners who crossed the racial divide and brought Americans together—even if only for brief moments—with melodies, rhythms and storytelling.

For the next few years, King's music continued to hit the R & B charts. He had a few number one hits, and he remained on the top twenty list for three years. If Robert Johnson sold his soul to the devil at the crossroads,

Friends Martha and B.B. King. From the Martha King Family Collection. *Courtesy of Mary Alice Smith.*

then B.B. King gave his heart to the musical highways. He traveled as often as the roadways, juke joints and dance halls would have him and was known as one of the hardest-working men in show business. In 1955, King formed a large band. The group was composed of sixteen people, including the Walker Brothers (Cato, King's bus driver, and King's bassist Shinny) and Evelyn "Mama Nuts" Young (saxophonist). Traveling to a gig called for an entourage of cars, so King purchased his first bus, which he dubbed "Big Red."

When B.B. King was in his early thirties, Sue Carol Hall, who was fifteen years old, caught his eye, and they fell in love. They enjoyed going fishing together. After a short courtship, King decided he wanted to marry Sue but had to wait until she turned eighteen. He married her in 1958 in a ceremony that was officiated by Aretha Franklin's father, the Reverend C.L. Franklin, in Detroit, Michigan. Sue's mother, Ruby Edwards, purchased Club Ebony in Indianola that same year. Unlike his first wife, Martha, who stayed at home while King toured, Sue packed up her suitcase and went on the road with him. They purchased a home in Los Angeles, and once Sue settled in, King went back on the road and hardly ever went home to rest his hat. He had a great yearning to share blues music—a desire that was ever increasing. King and Hall were married for less than ten years, and he fathered a number of children outside of their marriage during that time.

Journalist Gerri Hirshey referred to King as "the almighty rollingest stone." He was divorced from two wives and was a self-proclaimed "womanizer." He loved women.

7

THE BUSINESS OF MAKING MUSIC

Traveling on the road almost every day of the year can be tiring, dangerous and lonely. Tragedy struck in 1958 when B.B. King's tour bus, Big Red, collided with a butane truck on a bridge in Texas. King was not on the bus at that time, and no one on the bus was injured, but the driver of the butane truck was killed in the fiery wreck. As if that wasn't bad enough, the incident incurred a great deal of debt that took years for King to pay off because, as luck would have it, his insurance on the bus had been suspended a few days before the accident, making him personally liable. Things were bad for King at this time, but he continued performing.

King never gave up, and his tenacity paid off that same year when he recorded Joe Turner's song "Sweet Sixteen." It hit the charts in 1960 and became his signature tune. King's work ethic helped make him one of the most popular musicians in the world, though he had been paying his dues for many years.

Musicians love exploring their creativity, but most are not particularly fond of the business side of the performing arts. Income tax debt has destroyed the careers of many musicians. Black musicians have historically had a hard time, particularly during the early twentieth century when their music was placed in the hands of bad management that was either inexperienced, self-serving or both.

King's financial troubles followed him and caused him considerable uneasiness in 1966. There were times when he would stand on stage with his guitar, look out at the crowd and become suspicious of someone in the

B.B. King performing at Club Ebony. *Courtesy of Ralph Smith.*

audience. During one Chicago performance, he saw four white men in the audience and wondered if they were with the IRS. He thought they had come, not to hear him perform, but to deal with his tax issues.

Once a musician or screen actor gained a fanbase, people would take their recognition of the artist to another level. Television brought actors and musicians into homes, and at live performances, audiences could grow aggressive, screaming and wanting to get on stage to touch the artists. Musicians such as Mahalia Jackson, Cab Calloway and Little Richard all experienced this type of frenzy while performing.

The world was being introduced to B.B. King, but changes in how to handle business were a major consideration. It was not always easy to know which direction to take. In 1962, King changed record companies and booking agencies and signed on with the popular ABC Paramount. King was ready. When artists made this type of change, they hoped that their records would become household names for white audiences as well as black. It would take a few more years before King crossed over though. He was being represented by the New York firm Milt Shaw Booking Agency, and the executives were pleased to add his name to their roster. He was a hard-working musician who could potentially make a lot of money for the company and for himself.

King was on a roll, traveling the highways with block-booked performances (performances along the route) and performances that were scheduled over great distances. In 1963, "How Blue Can You Get," written by jazz critic Leonard Feather, became another hit. Even today, that song is recognized for the signature line, "I gave you seven children and now you wanna give 'em back." King was onto something. When he performed and recorded *Live at the Regal* in November 1964, it cemented his reputation as King of the Blues, a title that was his calling card until his death at the age of eighty-nine.

Looking at the lives of artists who have made it and are recognized as public figures can be interesting. Today's technology allows us to view an artist's early life and career and even magnify some of the intimate details of a more personal nature. Publicists have used the internet to present the polished, successful stars of today. It becomes even more interesting when we learn that they once looked like you and me. But with fame comes grooming and transformation. Between 1962 and 1964, ABC Paramount decided that B.B. King needed to make a change in his life and mirror other successful musicians. The label tried to create an image that they thought would help King cross over into the venues patronized by white audiences. The idea was to add violins to the band. Up to this point, that type of instrumentation had not been King's most successful offering.

Adding violin along with guitar would have caused some musicians to give up. Many would not have been able to afford to continue. Some would consider themselves failures because the music could have been perceived as a betrayal and cop-out to the purity of the blues sound. Artistic journeys are filled with hiccups along the way. Whether or not King knew to set a standard for himself and his music, one thing is evident: the music he brought out of the cotton fields and across the roadways of rural Mississippi transcended any minor speed bumps. For a while, violins were added to the background sound, but King instinctively knew that he needed to continue playing Lucille, and he needed to give his heart and soul to the blues and to his audiences.

When we see entertainers, they are often giving us a performance that exhibits quality and artistic excellence, but behind the mask there can be things going on in their personal lives that can take away their grit and gumption. In 1966, King's wife, Sue, divorced him. Worse still, his bus was stolen, and the IRS audited him and said that he owed $78,000 in back taxes. At the same time, King's blues journey continued to blossom. ABC Paramount created a new label and started recording King on BluesWay Records, which was a label dedicated to blues musicians.

Another significant event in King's career occurred when he recorded a live album in Chicago. Titled *Blues Is King*, it is still regarded as one of his finest recordings. He was virtually unknown to white audiences, but that was about to change and not just because he was out there performing. His vision for the blues was starting to take hold as listeners learned more about the genre. Around this time, Charles Keil's book *Urban Blues* was published, and it featured King as an example of the blues genre. Elektra Records promoted the Paul Butterfield Blues Band, a group that became an introduction for young, white fans to learn about the music. Elmore James and Little Walter Jacobs became favorites, and performers like Mike Bernard Bloomfield, former guitarist for the Paul Butterfield Blues Band, highlighted B.B. King as the master.

In 1967, at Café Au Go Go in New York, King jammed with Eric Clapton for the first time. Clapton, then a member of the group Cream and the Yardbirds, was only twenty-two. King was almost twenty years Clapton's senior, but they became friends and collaborated over the years. They were ahead of the times. They notably recorded "Rock Me Baby" in 1997. Clapton has received eighteen Grammy awards and has many other awards and accolades attached to his name.

King continued his musical journey, and in 1968, at the Fillmore West—once known as the Majestic Hall at 1805 Geary Boulevard—in San Francisco, the audience cheered enthusiastically as he stepped onto the stage. In fact, he received three or four standing ovations, an experience that greatly humbled him. He was so touched that the majority-white crowd would do that for him. His mind flashed back to the days of segregation, and he reflected on how much had changed. Having long believed that music was the balm that could heal racial divides, it was his dream come true to take it all in after performing for segregated audiences for so long and plowing a pathway through the civil rights era.

About this transformation in society, King said,

> *I grew up in a segregated society and I learned I can get things done much better by talking to a person with an even temperament. I find just talkin' straight to a person, giving them the facts, they usually pay attention and listen at least somewhat….That's how I stayed out of devilment back in the segregated days. I would speak as I felt, but not in anger, even though the insides of me were tearin' apart. My mom taught me that. I remember when she was dyin'…she said to me, "If you'll always be nice to people, there will always be somebody who will stand up for you." She wasn't lyin'*

at all....It's no secret that it was a pattern in all the Southern parts of the country. What you might not know is that the same thing happened in many other parts of the country when we toured in the beginning. You're gonna find that, as long as we live, it's gonna be a part of life. But discriminating against people because of their color, creed, religion, etc., could be corrected more than it is.

This was still a season of change in B.B. King's life. After squabbling over money with his business manager, King decided it was time to call it quits. He hired Sidney Seidenberg as his new manager. Seidenberg was an experienced accountant who sometimes booked gigs that were not as lucrative to get King more exposure. It turned out to be the best thing that he could have done at the time. In 1968, King signed on with Associated Booking Corporation, a company that managed two well-known musicians, Louis Armstrong and Antoine "Fats" Domino. Between 1969 and 1971, Seidenberg helped B.B. King get his name known to the masses. In November 1969, when the Rolling Stones came to the United States on tour, B.B. King had an opportunity to perform with them. The group had been playing primarily to all-white audiences, and King opened for them on at least eighteen engagements across the country. Other well-known entertainers who toured with the Rolling Stones included Chuck Berry, Janis Joplin and Ike and Tina Turner.

"The Thrill Is Gone" made King a legend. When he appeared on the *Ed Sullivan Show*, millions of viewers had an opportunity to see and hear him. The show aired from 1948 to 1971 and was a household name. Hardly anyone in the United States missed it. Sullivan regularly hosted rising stars and new performers, and there was no doubt that viewers were in for a treat on Sunday nights. Remarkably, Seidenberg got King on the show at the same time as Tony Bennett, George Burns, the Carpenters and a few other acts on October 18, 1970. It was a stroke of genius. King had hoped for an opportunity to talk with Sullivan and maybe shake his hand. Sadly, that didn't happen. But King never let small slights like that keep him from moving toward his goal. He went from mostly playing in all-black clubs to performing in larger venues for white audiences.

In 1971, King went on his first overseas tour to London to record with the Rolling Stones. They recorded their first collaborative album, *B.B. King in London*, with various British rock and R & B artists.

Over the years, B.B. King performed, toured and recorded with some of the greatest musicians in the world, such as Bobby "Blue" Bland, Bono and U2. He has entertained queens, kings and presidents. Continuing to travel the roadway to success, in 1971, King received his first Grammy: Best Rhythm and Blues Vocal Performance (male) for "The Thrill Is Gone." He was invited to appear on television shows, such as the *Merv Griffin Show*, which was another popular program that showcased what was trending at the time.

Though he is known for his music, King was also an active advocate. He performed in Sing Sing Correctional Facility, a maximum-security prison in Ossining, New York. He advocated for fairer prison conditions by co-founding the Foundation for the Advancement of Inmate Recreation and Rehabilitation (FAIRR). He was honored for his efforts with the Humanitarian Award from the Federal Bureau of Prisons in 1972. B.B. King was a remarkable and generous man, but there are other stories about his life that have taken front seat to the stories of his humanitarian efforts.

People were interested in King's music and personal life. In 1980, journalist Charles Sawyer wrote the first biography on King's life, called *The Arrival of B.B. King*. It was as if King stepped out of a royal carriage and onto major stages—an impression due in part to his connections with other artists whose stars were also rising. As a result, King started receiving invitations from such artists as U2 to go on world tours. Not only did he tour with much younger, but equally talented, musicians, he also recorded with them, and those collaborations helped to expand the world's understanding and knowledge of the blues. In 1988, he recorded "When Loves Comes to Town" with U2. Prior to recording with B.B. King, the group had just been recognized for their own music with the album *The Joshua Tree*, which was released in 1987.

King also toured and recorded with Gary Moore, a Northern Irish guitarist who was known to share the stage with newcomers. He also performed with the Muddy Shoes, a group of musicians from Hungary who revitalized the music of Gertrude "Ma" Rainey with the reintroduction of her early twentieth-century song "Black-Eyed Blues." And there were others. It is said that the British musicians were a "beacon of light," showing high regard for King's music, which raised awareness around the world for blues. These collaborations also showed that King had the ability to adapt and work with different styles of music. He was a consummate and masterful artist. When talking with young musicians, he never forgot how he got his start.

B.B. King encouraged everyone he met to keep doing their best work and to never give up because of feelings of defeat, mistakes or setbacks. No matter where you go in this world, if you ever meet anyone who has met the King—young or old—they will tell you a story of how he shared a good

Above: B.B. King and Kristen Dupard, the 2012 Poetry Out Loud National Champion. *Courtesy of Susan Liles.*

Left: Nancy Davison and B.B. King. *Courtesy of Mary Alice Smith.*

Kishna Anderson and B.B. King. *Courtesy of Mary Alice Smith.*

word of cheer, and they will tell you that he showed interest in his fellow man. He was a humanitarian and a philanthropist. As someone who knew the blues as a way of rising above one's circumstances, he knew how to sing a melody that could make you smile. When the King played the blues, the lyrics would send out the call, and his guitar would respond by echoing and reverberating a powerful testimony to his life.

Some of his best advice was,

I would say to all people, but maybe to young people especially—black and white or whatever color—follow your own feelings and trust them, find out what you want to do and do it, and then practice it every day of your life and keep becoming what you are, despite any hardships and obstacles you meet.

PART II

Family Recollections

8

SHIRLEY KING

B.B. King's Daughter

King is not a star. B.B. King is a moon. Stars can burn out, but moons never do.
—Rufus Thomas

Shirley's father never married any of his children's mothers, but Shirley said that he gave her his last name: King. He took her in at two and a half years old and placed her with his family. Shirley was born on October 26, 1949. Of all the children B.B. King claimed, she is the third oldest living now, with only one boy who is older than her. (Little B.B. King, who is mentioned later in this book, claims to also be the son of B.B. King, but most documents do not reference him as being one of King's fifteen children.)

Originally from Arkansas, Shirley claims Tennessee as her home as well. Her mother, Mary Elizabeth Gilmer, née Jackson, is from West Memphis, Arkansas. B.B. King always called her Liz. Mary Elizabeth married another man two years after Shirley was born. Shirley's stepfather was a little put off with B.B. King coming around, but her parents were always good friends, so they thought it would be best for Shirley to go and live with her family. Shirley said that her father always knew how to do things right so that no one would get hurt. She said that his life was built on honesty, and he believed you should do unto others as you would have them do unto you. He always told his children he loved them when he came home.

Mary Elizabeth was always a little jealous when she was with King because he was very popular with the women. She knew what she wanted—she was not one of those hangers-on. She saw that he liked his life with a lot of women, and she wanted her life with just one man, so they agreed to break up. But King committed to do the right thing for his daughter.

When Mary Elizabeth had a problem, King was always there to make sure everything was all right, even after she married another man. When her husband was involved in an accident and she had other children to care for, King assisted the family. Shirley said that only a real man would do what her father, B.B. King, did. When Mary Elizabeth's husband was disabled after the accident, King would bring groceries for the entire family. That was the kind of man he was. Shirley lauded her father by saying that he was the most amazing man she had ever met in her life. He was "one of a kind," she said. He brought a carload of things the family needed. Although it was a bit awkward for Shirley's stepfather, it did take some of the pressure off him. There are not very many men who would leave a woman behind, then come back and look out for her concerns when something happens.

Mary Elizabeth had six other children, but Shirley was the oldest. Mary Elizabeth always respected B.B. King, and if Shirley ever got upset with him, she would remind her daughter that he was a good man and that she should always love him. King, in turn, would always say positive things about Mary Elizabeth. After King moved his daughter in with his family, he always asked her how her mother was doing, and she felt bad because she had become part of his family and his world and had not stayed in touch with her mother as much. Her father became her world. Even though she loved her mother, she felt like she really needed her father in her life.

When she stayed with King's family, she was living in the home with King's father, Albert Lee King, and his wife, Ada. When King became successful, he bought the family a house on Hubert Street in Memphis. As of this writing, his stepbrother is still living there. That was the first house B.B. King purchased when he started making money. A giver all his life, he didn't just buy himself a car, he bought his stepsister one too. He was always doing things like that.

When she was seventeen, Shirley moved to Chicago to live with relatives on her mother's side of the family. She continued to have opportunities to be around her father and his family, such as when he performed in Chicago around 1967. She watched her father go from place to place, even when others started managing him and telling him where to go.

King's other children didn't have the same opportunity to live around their father and his family like Shirley. They came into the picture later. She thought she was the only child, but as she grew older, she started hearing about other children. Her father felt that he should take care of all his children. Albert King told his son that if he was told that he fathered a child, then they were his to care for. He didn't worry about paternity tests back then, but when the number of children escalated, he decided to cut it off and stopped acknowledging the possibility that he was someone's child's father, Shirley said.

Shirley felt that having her dad in her life was comparable to having Jesus Christ in her life. She said that she is in church and that she knows Jesus Christ, and her father was the closest person she had ever met who helped her understand the love of Christ. Even when people were unkind or unfair to her dad, Shirley said that he kept being Mr. Nice Guy. It seems he kept doing what his mother had taught him. Shirley never understood how her father could keep turning the other cheek. He told her, "If you live in this world and you love people and treat them the way that you want to be treated, you are always going to be blessed." And that did happen for him.

Shirley is a singer like her father and said that her audiences feel a connection to her dad's spirit when she performs. She loves it because she knows that she inherited some of her talent from him. He would always tell her how pretty she was and that she was special. Shirley has a background as a dancer, and she appeared in the 1976 movie *The Human Tornado*, an action/comedy drama directed by Cliff Roquemore, staring Rudy Ray Moore.

In December 2014, a few months prior to her father's passing, she felt like a little girl when he told her that he was proud of her. She asked him for a special gift. She wanted one of his coats, and he gave it to her. King believed in holding on to gifts people gave him, but he wanted Shirley to know she had stepped out on faith and had become the person she was on her own—without holding on to his coattails. She now realizes that he was telling her to "be who you are so that if I'm not around you can still be that person." She said that sometimes when you are riding on people's coattails and they go down, you go down with them. Her father always had a way of teaching her lessons that would take her a little while to figure out. In the end, she realized that he would build her and others up because he had to do that for himself when he had no family around to raise and take care of him. He had to become a man at nine to ten years old, so he knew how to teach others to become independent.

Shirley said that she learned most of what she knows about her father from reading about him in books. He was on the road all the time and didn't sit around talking about his life when he went home. In December 2014, during the last few months of his life, Shirley might have gotten more of her

Shirley King and Diane Williams at the Blue Biscuit Restaurant in Indianola, Mississippi. *Courtesy of Glynn Fought.*

father's attention if he had not been so sick. She didn't want to press him for information at that time, but she didn't know that would be the last time she would see her father alive.

Shirley learned from reading a book about her father that when he was a child, he started trusting the birds to be his friends because he didn't have any brothers or sisters. His half-siblings only came into the picture when his father remarried. Shirley feels that it hurt B.B. King to sit around talking about the things that happened in his life. When he would talk about his mother, you could tell that he never stopped missing her. Shirley also found out about B.B. King's younger brother, Curce, by reading books about his life.

Shirley was proud that her father spent nine decades on earth and that he worked hard the entire time.

9

MARY ALICE SMITH

Martha's Daughter

B.B. King was the first husband of Mary Alice Smith's mother. Her mother was Martha Lee Denton. Mary Alice said that her mother was "crazy" about B.B. King, and he was crazy about her. They married when he was nineteen and she was eighteen. They picked cotton together when they were young and married in November 1944. (Mary Alice said that she has a copy of the marriage certificate listing the date, though most accounts say they married in 1946 when King was twenty-one. Charles Sawyer, project consultant for the B.B. King Museum, included the year 1944 in his timeline of B.B. King's life.) When her mother told her and her siblings about the relationship, they were all excited to learn that their mother had been married to someone famous. Martha told her daughter that she had twins by King, but they both died very young. Mary Alice has an older brother, and her mother never explicitly told her that he is King's son, but Mary Alice believes that he is. When she met some of the other King family members and showed them pictures of her mother, her brother and B.B. King, the family asked about the resemblance of her brother to King. Everyone was surprised to learn about her brother Danny Davison.

King's sister, Fay, told Mary Alice that Martha had confided to her that she did indeed have a son by King, but she didn't want anyone to know. In 2005, King went to Illinois for a performance at the Genesee Theatre in downtown Waukegan. Martha, Mary Alice, her sister, and Mary Alice's daughter went downtown to see him. They talked with King on his tour bus, and Martha and B.B. reminisced about how they met and married. King

Danny Davison and Mary Alice Smith. Some say Danny looks like B.B. *Courtesy of Mary Alice Smith.*

told Martha that she had beautiful daughters, and he invited them to go with him to Las Vegas. She told King that her eldest son was his child, and King told her to go ahead and get the DNA test. King was willing to do the test so Martha could have peace of mind about the secret she had been keeping for so long. No DNA test was ever conducted

Mary Alice lights up when she talks about her older brother. Anyone who has seen her brother testifies that he must be one of King's sons because he looks so much like him. Mary Alice met B.B. King's daughter Shirley when she and her husband picked her up in Chicago so they could drive to Mississippi together for King's funeral. Shirley and Mary Alice shared a lot during that time, and Shirley expressed her love for Mary Alice and the other children. Shirley had previously met Mary Alice's mother, Martha, and had interaction with her from time to time.

Martha told Mary Alice about the times when King would go off to perform, and she confided in her daughter that she was jealous because she thought he was cheating on her with other women. When B.B. King was married and living with Martha, he enjoyed everything about her, and he told her so. He liked her physical attributes, including her smile, her walk and her figure. He loved the way she cooked, and he always enjoyed buying nice things for her. They did a lot together when they were married. They didn't have much money growing up or when they first got married, so Martha worked outside of the home to help earn money. In all, Martha had seven children. Danny is the oldest of the boys and Mary Alice is the oldest of the girls, and if it is true that Danny is King's son, then he would be the oldest of all of King's children. Mary Alice met King's other children at his funeral in May 2015.

Mary Alice said that now that King is gone, many people come to her because King was her mother's first husband. They ask a lot of questions, such as, "Are they going to make a movie, and will the children be in the

Left: Diane Davison and B.B. King. *Courtesy of Mary Alice Smith.*

Below: Mary Kay Davison and B.B. King. *Courtesy of Mary Alice Smith.*

movie?" When asked about what she would say about him, Mary Alice simply said that he was a loving person. If he had anything, he would give it to the whole world. Mary Alice said that when she first met him, she "just loved him so much," and her mother "never wanted for anything" because of his generosity. If Martha needed something or if she was sick, she would have her daughter call King's secretary, and he would send her whatever she needed.

When Mary Alice was asked to describe her mother and what she meant to her, she said her mother was "the most beautiful woman in the world" to her and her siblings. Martha loved to cook and clean and made sure that her children ate breakfast, lunch and dinner. She was crazy about King.

Martha and B.B. King's marriage certificate from the Martha King Family Collection. *Courtesy of Mary Alice Smith.*

Danny Davison and Mary Alice Smith, Martha King's children. *Courtesy of Mary Alice Smith.*

She would do anything for him, and he would do anything for her. But she wanted a good husband. She talked about him constantly, and the children were mesmerized with the references she would make to the musician. Mary Alice said everyone in the family is still excited about the relationship. It was an honor that King wrote a song about Martha. Mary Alice believes that at least three or four of King's songs were about her mother. She said that she knew that the song "Sweet Sixteen" was one of his favorites and that it may have been a reference to her mother.

10

MARVIN GARDNER

Little B.B. King

Upon introduction, he will tell you that his name is "Marvin King, son of the legendary blues guitarist and singer B.B. King." Marvin, born November 14, 1943, said that he didn't know that B.B. King was his father until he was in his forties and his mother, on her deathbed, told him so. He asked his mother why she did not tell him before, and she said it was because she got married to someone else. Marvin was a baby when she got married, and she couldn't tell her husband because he had accepted Marvin as his child.

When he learned about King being his father, Marvin started following him. He went to Mississippi and had a chance to meet King. He decided not to reveal what his mother told him at that time. In 1998, he called the Indianola Chamber of Commerce and asked if they knew when King would be in town. He was told that King would be there June 2. Marvin went down to see King and told him what his mother had said. King's response was, "Your mother is right. I was going to tell you eventually."

Marvin always loved the way King played guitar. He listened to the blues on his mother's old gramophone when he was young, and guitar music would always send chills throughout his body when he heard "the scream in it." He always told his mother that he "wanted to be like that man," but he didn't know at the time that King was his daddy. She would always say, "One day, maybe you'll be like him." Since then, Marvin had a chance to perform with his father in Mississippi.

He was asked by someone at a television station in Mississippi, "What makes you like the blues so much?" He responded that it was "being born black in the South." He has a Lucille guitar that looks exactly like King's, and he even had King's name printed on the guitar's neck. He purchased the guitar for $3,300 and had it inlaid with ten carat gold.

When asked what impressed him about the blues, Marvin said that blues music is storytelling music about the struggles of everyday life. If a baby cried because it wanted a bottle, or a man got angry because his girlfriend or wife left him for no reason that he could think of—that's the blues. Marvin said that he remembers dropping a biscuit on the floor, and that gave him the blues because he really wanted to eat that biscuit.

Marvin said that King told him the blues is the basic rule of life. King told him, "I'm not always going to be here." According to Marvin, King would never say "the Lord" or "God" or "Jesus" or anything like that. He would say, "When the Almighty power above calls me, I want you to continue the legacy of playing the blues."

Marvin would start to respond, "I think I…" But he said that King would say, "Don't tell me what you think, just do it!" Marvin told him that he "thought" he could do it. But King said to him, "If you weren't good enough, you wouldn't be able to stand up and perform with me," and King would chuckle. Marvin said he made that promise to King, and he is doing his best to continue. He feels good when he is performing—like his father is smiling on him. Marvin also said that people have told him he looks like King when he performs. Maybe it is the way he turns or tilts his head, or maybe it is the way he closes his eyes, but there is a resemblance to King's style in Marvin's gestures. Marvin said that when he performs, his guitar tells him the next lyrics, and it tells him, "Let me sing it a while and you come back in later." He plays twelve, fourteen or sixteen bars, then comes back in with his voice. At that point, "It seems then that both of us are satisfied."

Marvin was only thirteen years old when he started playing the guitar. In an interview at the Elks Club in Pensacola, Florida, in 2016, Marvin, who was in his seventies, said his sister, Sandra, encouraged him to write a book about his life. He said he didn't have time to write because he traveled so much around the country and overseas, and when he comes back home, he goes fishing. He enjoys taking his boat up the river near his home in Georgia. Other than that, he spends most of his time playing music.

Marvin said that he performed at Club Ebony on the evening of King's funeral in May 2015. Riley Jr. was always thought to be the oldest son of

B.B. King, but Marvin has staked claim to that title. In his performances, he bills himself as "Little B.B. King, son of the legendary King of the Blues."

At the time of this writing, a DNA test has not been conducted to confirm that Marvin is King's biological son. The children who have been widely recognized as B.B. King's children as listed in the obituary during King's funeral in Indianola are:

Barbara Clark (deceased)
Leonard King (deceased)
Gloria King (deceased)
Riletta Mitchell (deceased)
Ruby Davis
Robert Edwards
Riley King Jr.
Patty King
Willie King
Claudette (Robinson) King
Michelle (Seroy) King
Rita Washington
Karen Williams
Barbara Winfree
Shirley (Peterson) King

PART III

Let Them Talk but Hear What They've Got to Say

Interviews with Music Makers Who Were Influenced by B.B. King

We need more of him.
—Bobby Bland

The people interviewed in this section of the book have agreed to share their personal recollections, reflections and impressions of the blues; memories of B.B. King; and the ways in which he impacted the music industry and influenced their lives. The following interviews received minor edits.

11

MALCOLM SHEPHERD

Percussionist and President, Central Mississippi Blues Society

Malcolm Shepherd is the current president of the Central Mississippi Blues Society. He reflected on the organization's mission to bring blues to the community by producing the show Blue Monday on Monday nights at Hal & Mal's restaurant in Jackson for more than ten years. Singer Dorothy Moore is a frequent visitor to the show, as are musicians Bobby Rush, Eddie Cotton Jr. and Grady Champion. On any Monday night, you might hear three or four featured guitarists and eight or nine other musicians during the open mic session. International visitors come all the time, and several artists have been discovered on Blue Monday nights. The society is committed to keeping the blues alive and continuing the legacy of B.B. King.

The Central Mississippi Blues Society is chartered by the International Blues Foundation out of Memphis and sponsors programs such as Blues in the Park, where musicians jam in the parks around Jackson. It also sponsors a program called Blues in the Schools, and the foundation's recommended curriculum is used to teach math, science, geography and history to young people of all ages.

Malcolm Shepherd has been in the music industry for most of his life. He is a percussionist and singer of R & B, blues and gospel. His father was a gospel and blues singer and his sister Jewel Bass is a local blues recording artist. She was the first woman to represent Mississippi in the black beauty pageant. Shepherd's other sisters, Betty and Irene, are also gospel singers. He said that he can go back to his great-great-grandmother to chart his family's involvement with music. He has another reason to keep the blues alive: It is one of the great American art forms that blacks have given to the world.

As previously discussed, there is a long battle going on between blues and gospel. It really isn't a fight, but people have characterized the blues as the devil's music and gospel as spiritual or God's music, though the actual compositions are the same. In many cases, the music you hear on Sunday morning is the same music you hear on Saturday night with a few word changes. On Saturday night, it is "oh, baby," and on Sunday morning it is "oh, Lord," but the rhythms and chords stay the same.

In considering the metamorphosis of the blues, Shepherd said that most people think of traditional blues or roots music that was performed with an acoustic guitar. Sometimes the guitar was amplified, but it still had that acoustic sound. That was the first stage, as played by Robert Johnson and Tommy Johnson. There are people who will say the blues tell a sad story, but that's not always true. The blues also talk about accomplishment, while couched in an environment that is both relatable and acceptable to the people who listen to it. As Shepherd reflected on the origins of blues, "During those days, slaves were not allowed to have hand drums in their quarters. They couldn't have a djembe or any other type of drum." Consequently, if you listen to acoustic guitar players from back in the day, or if you are lucky enough to see them on film, you will find that in lieu of a drum, they would slap on the guitar to keep the beat. A further metamorphosis came about when the acoustic players turned their attention to electric guitars wired up to capture the entire sound that came out of the instrument. To hear the guitar, it had to be plugged into an amplifier. The resulting effect was a much louder guitar. The sound could be heard across an open field. Changing the nature of the blues with an electric guitar, musicians could use synthesizers and wah-wahs, and they could bend notes further than they could with an acoustic guitar.

Some people would take issue with Shepherd because there are some acoustic guitar players whose skill would make you think the guitar is electrified. In truth, the electric guitar did change the whole nature of the music. Some call it urban blues, when the pace of the music picked up. That's when B.B. King, Howlin' Wolf, Muddy Waters and that whole second tier of blues performers came about. They all left Mississippi because they had to get away from what was called traditional blues—and along came Stax Records in Memphis, Tennessee.

For a while, Chicago and Detroit and the urban sound of the blues took over because there was a larger market for it. Now you have just a few of those musicians left, such as King Edward (Antoine), Bobby Rush and Jesse Robinson. B.B. King based his music on the roots music of Tommy Johnson and Robert Johnson. Now there is a third tier of blues artists—Eddie Cotton Jr., Grady Champion and Jarekus Singleton—who didn't grow up with roots music, but instead they grew up listening to King and others like him. If you listen to their music, you will seldom hear the slow-tempo blues commonly played on the acoustic guitar.

The blues are changing, not only based on the instrumentation, but also based on the generation and times that we live in. You don't hear people talking about how hard it is in the field picking cotton anymore, nor will you hear the songs of Muddy Waters and those guys who said, "I'll never go back to picking cotton again." Now what you are hearing is music that is more urban oriented. Younger guys are coming along, and they have listened very well. They may play the cover tunes from B.B. King, Elmore James and others from that era rather than reaching back and playing what Tommy Johnson or Robert Johnson played.

Shepherd went on to say that B.B. King was probably the best of all the blues musicians who came out of that era. Shepherd met with him several times, including an encounter at King's club in Indianola years ago. The

Inside Club Ebony. *Courtesy of Susan Liles.*

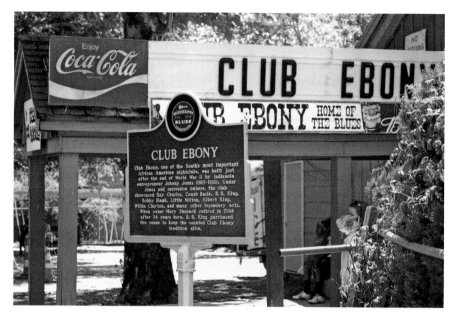

Outside Club Ebony in Indianola, Mississippi. *Courtesy of Susan Liles.*

last time Shepherd saw him was at the homecoming festival just after the B.B. King Museum opened. He said that B.B. King never got superstar syndrome. He would stop and talk with anybody. He was very encouraging to everybody, even when he heard someone who couldn't play very well. He wouldn't say, "You need to give it up." He would just tell them to keep on playing. He was not only a great musician; he was a great human being as well.

When other musicians messed up, B.B. King would always tell them, "It's all right." Those were his words: "It's all right. Just keep on playing." He was a welcoming and encouraging person.

The blues musicians of today are still capturing the culture of the blues, and as long as they keep doing that, the blues will never die, and B.B. King will still be around us—in our hearts and in our minds.

12

BOBBY RUSH

Blues Entertainer

orn Emmett Ellis Jr., Bobby Rush changed his name because his best friend, his father, was a preacher. His father was his biggest inspiration. If it weren't for his father, Rush thinks that he wouldn't be singing the blues today. He never prevented Rush from singing the blues, which was a green light for the young boy. If his father had said not to sing the blues, Rush wouldn't be singing today because of the respect he had for him.

When Rush was a little boy, his cousin gave him a guitar, but he hid it in a loft because he thought his father wouldn't want him to have it. A week or two later, his father came to him and said, "Boy, bring me that guitar." Emmett was afraid and marveled at how his father knew he had it; it seemed to him that his father and mother knew almost everything. He brought the guitar to his father, and he tuned it and said, "Let me sing you a song, boy. I used to sing it when I was a little older than you are now." Now, his father had no intention of singing a gospel song. They both looked toward the kitchen and assumed that his mother was out of earshot. Then his father said, "I'm going to sing you a song about what me and this woman used to do." Emmett was itching to find out what his father had done, but he didn't know how to ask. He just listened as his father sang:

Me and my gal went chinkapen hunting,
She fell down, and I saw something.

Emmett said, "Daddy!" He was looking for a gospel song, but this was different. "Daddy. Sing it again!" He wanted his father to sing the next verse. He knew that a chinkapen was like a small pecan, but he also knew that if the song said, "She fell down, and I saw something," then in the next verse his father would tell him what it was that he saw. Emmett was too young and naïve to ask. He was around seven or eight years old at the time. He said, "Sing it again!" His father sang:

Me and my gal went chinkapen hunting,
She fell down and I saw something.

That was funny to Emmett. He asked his daddy how big she was. Without even a hint of a smile, his father responded by saying that the girl was "real fat." Now Emmett had more information. He asked his dad, "What did she have on?" His father said, "Nothing but a dress."

Emmett's mind was racing. He really wanted to ask his dad what he saw. He asked his dad to sing the song again. At this point, his mother cleared her throat and declared that "men don't sing that type of song to their boys." His father did so anyway, apparently thinking that Emmett's mother wouldn't hear him this time, but he didn't see her coming up behind him.

When he started singing again, Emmett said, "Daddy, here comes Muh." His father went to singing again, but sang the song differently this time:

Me and my gal went chinkapen hunting,
She fell down, and I kept running.

Emmett never learned the rest of the song, but in this way, his father gave him his first lesson in the blues. As time passed, he grew to love blues music, and as an entertainer, he looked for a name that wouldn't embarrass his father. Nowadays, everybody calls him Bobby Rush, a name he came up with early in his career. If someone calls him Bobby, he won't answer. If somebody calls him Rush, he won't answer. He wants to be called Bobby Rush. It's his brand.

Out of all the entertainers Rush has met, he thinks B.B. King is one of the most impressive. As an artist, King stood still while everyone else moved in different directions, either trying to find themselves or trying to be in line with what was happening at the time. When disco came in, Rush and others went in that direction for a while, but King stood still. King didn't change, even when the going was rough. He had to survive like everyone else, but he stayed dominant with his phrasing and his signature style.

Bobby Rush has performed with famous musicians, such as Chuck Berry, Little Richard and Fats Domino, but those shows were different than the ones he did with B.B. King. He performed with King 180 times during his career, including when Charles Evers booked them for the Medgar Evers Festival. He has even been on the same program with King and Count Basie (1959–60). Back then, Rush didn't think much about it. He considered King to be a friend like any other musician he had worked with, and he took those opportunities for granted. According to Rush, King was a kind person. Whether he liked you or not, you couldn't tell because he was so kind, and even if you caught him at a bad time, he would still ask how you were doing.

Bobby Rush was named King of the Chitlin' Circuit by *Rolling Stone* magazine because he was one of the few musicians who had a big enough following to go beyond the circuit. Yet Rush was "never too big in the head" to come back to the circuit and perform for a two-hundred-seat audience when he could have been performing in Europe for more than twenty thousand people instead. He did these shows because there were people who wanted to see him who couldn't afford the more expensive venues. Rush could choose his shows because he always managed himself and controlled what he did. He feels that B.B. King desired to do the same thing, but it was out of his control because of his management. Today, Rush believes that King's management always pushed King out there. That's a good thing, but once your price goes up, it pulls you away from the Chitlin' Circuit.

The Chitlin' Circuit was known as a musical avenue for black people. According to Rush, white folks named it because it was all about "black people in little juke joints," but that's not where the name really comes from. Rather, in the early 1950s, when Rush was working in Pine Bluff, Arkansas, in a place called Jitterbugs, they cooked chitterlings every day. He was making twelve dollars per week, which was big money—his previous jobs paid sixteen dollars per month. At Jitterbugs, they would fry or boil chitterlings and fix them up for the musicians to eat. Instead of being paid in cash for their shows, the musicians ate free.

Rush recalled that prior to the 1950s, chitterlings were given away at the slaughterhouses—they weren't sold until it was realized that black people saw them as a food staple. When the food became popular, the industry started selling them in grocery stores. The juke joints along the circuit would seat as many as one hundred or two hundred people and sometimes as few as ten to fifteen. According to Rush, the Chitlin' Circuit is still around, but there are just not as many venues today.

Someone once asked him, "Bobby Rush, out of all the festivals you have worked, why don't more blacks attend blues festivals? Instead, we see more whites in attendance." Bobby said that oftentimes the ticket prices are too high for black audiences, and the festival organizers don't hire the kind of musicians that blacks want to see performing. If they want to see black people there, they hire artists such as Al Green.

Bobby Rush observed that even the music award events seem to leave out the blues. Blues awards were not recognized until white people started playing the blues. Another example of how music is not inclusive can be seen in the lack of reggae music awards because white folks are not making that type of music. There are plenty of music categories, but if it is all about a black category, the genre may be overlooked. We now have a rap category because white folks are buying it, and white folks are loving it. If it is just blacks loving the genre, there traditionally won't be an award category. Bobby Rush said that he doesn't want to linger on black and white issues, but the issues are alive and well.

Rush said that he is one of the few performers to cross over the color line, meaning that he has both black and white audiences. He said that there are few black performers like him who have crossed over. Some may cross over, but they generally won't have a black audience. In his experience, Rush saw 90 percent whites come to Indianola for the annual B.B. King Homecoming events. Yet when King passed away and was recognized at a memorial in Memphis, 90 percent of the attendees paying their respects were black. That hurt Rush because black people didn't support King while he lived, only when he passed away. What was more, the whites withdrew when he died. If he had gone to Memphis three months before King's passing, he imagines there would have been 90 percent white people in attendance at a gig. It hurts Bobby Rush that black folks were the ones who gave King his start, yet they didn't support him. Rush doesn't know why this happened, but he does know that there will never be another B.B. King. He said that when white musicians do the same thing as black musicians, it seems to put a value on it that was not there before. He went on to share an idiom: "You have to beware of a bear with a monkey's head." In other words, just because people say they love you, it doesn't mean they do. And just because they say they don't love you; it doesn't mean they don't.

When Rush played with Muddy Waters and J.B. Lenoir, they worked day in and day out behind drawn curtains. This was early in his career, pre–civil

B.B. King Homecoming Festival in Indianola, Mississippi. *Courtesy of Susan Liles.*

B.B. King Homecoming stage in Indianola, Mississippi. *Courtesy of Susan Liles.*

rights. The patrons wanted to hear their music, but they didn't want to see the musicians' faces. It was a joke to Waters and Lenoir, but it wasn't funny to Rush, even though black musicians were getting paid more money than they had ever made in their lives. Rush was earning $7.50 per night, and Waters was making $5.00 per night. Rush was making more money than the others because he was the band leader.

In the 1950s, Rush opened a show for Elvis Presley at a college. The producers drew a circle on the floor, and a string was hung from the ceiling to the floor, lining up with the circle. You couldn't see the string from the audience because it was a black haywire string, like the ones used for baling hay. The black musicians were not allowed to touch the string—if they shook their hips while performing, the producers would know. Rush said that every time his hips would touch the string, money would be docked from the full amount that he had been promised.

Rush also remembers when he first heard the word *integration*. When he was a young musician, he was playing in Chicago at a club where he was required to perform out of sight, unseen by the audience. He had to hear the word three times before he realized the club wanted to put him on the stage, so the audience could see him. This was unheard of at the time. In this sense, B.B. King paved the way for African American musicians. Rush struggled through those years, working on his own and paying dues, whereas King's management catapulted him above the struggles most musicians experienced in those days.

Bobby Rush uses the word *mortified* when he refers to his music today, but he went on to say that he sings blues just like John Lee Hooker and B.B. King sang the blues. He says that he has mortified his blues so that young people can relate to what he is doing. At this stage in life, he doesn't have to do what he did in the past because he is a household name. Noting that there is a difference between an entertainer and musician, he said you can teach a man to be a musician, and you can teach a man to play a guitar, but you can't really teach a man to do what he does. Rush believes that he was born to do what he does, and King was born to do what he did. There are plenty of guys who are great musicians who play in bands, but there's a difference. The pianist who played with Muddy Waters was a musician, but Waters was born to do what he did: entertain! You can't manufacture an Elvis Presley. Howlin' Wolf was also an entertainer, and he had many musicians who performed with him who were better musicians than he was. According to Rush, young people need to know the difference between an entertainer and a musician. A guitar player who sings is different from a singer who plays guitar. B.B. King was a mirror to Bobby Rush, he said, because what he saw in B.B. King, he sees in himself.

Bobby Rush was nominated for three Grammys. His 1971 hit "Chicken Heads" became his first gold record and re-entered the billboard charts thirty years after its second release, in the film *Black Snake Moan*. Rush's *Porcupine Meat* took home the Grammy Award for Best Traditional Blues Album in 2017. He appeared in the film *The Road to Memphis*, produced by Martin Scorsese. In fifty years of relentless touring and colorful live shows, he has performed all over the world—even at the White House, with James Brown, when President Bill Clinton was in office.

13

BILLY BRANCH

"Son of the Blues"

B illy Branch is an Emmy Award winner and three-time Grammy nominee who performs with a group called Billy Branch and the Sons of the Blues. Branch has been playing professionally for forty years and has had the good fortune to be mentored by some of the greatest musicians in the business. His most notable influence was Willie Dixon, in whose band he played for six years. Branch acknowledges Dixon as one of the most prolific composers in the world. A great philosopher and mentor, Dixon wrote hundreds of songs for other artists, including Howlin' Wolf, Little Walter, Sonny Boy Williamson and Muddy Waters. His most notable compositions are well-known tunes, such as "Hoochie Coochie," "Back Door Man" and "Wang Dang Doodle."

Branch was a student of Sterling Plumpp at the University of Illinois and has said that Plumpp has one of the most analytical and knowledgeable minds about the blues. Plumpp, a recognized poet, was often in attendance when Branch performed, and he told Branch that his playing was greatly impacted by being a member of Dixon's band. Branch said that Plumpp, who was originally from Mississippi, was the only black intellectual to chronicle the Chicago blues culture. Together, the two performed a unique blend of poetic recitation with intertwining harmonic melodies.

Branch has found the blues to be the most powerful music on the planet, affirming that it is a universal genre that describes a feeling that everyone has experienced at one time or another. There have been hundreds of first- and second-generation blues musicians, many of whom are now gone. A longtime observer of musicians such as Koko Taylor, Lonnie Brooks, Junior Wells, James Cotton and B.B. King, Branch will tell you that the blues will never die, despite many people's projections to the contrary.

Branch is known as an accomplished harmonica player, and like many musicians who are dedicated to the art, Branch teaches a Blues in Schools program. He has been teaching the course and talking about the history and culture of the Mississippi Delta for years, but he didn't get to see the Delta until Sade Turnipseed of Khafre Incorporated brought him to Indianola to speak with hundreds of students. During the weeks surrounding the opening of the B.B. King Museum, Branch taught the Blues in Schools program in Mississippi, a program he has been teaching since 1978.

For the opening of the museum, Turnipseed asked Branch to teach the children to play one of B.B. King's own songs, "King's Special." The goal was to have the children march to the museum while playing the song on the harmonica. The song was not intended for the harmonica, but he was determined to make it work. In preparation for the event, Branch created an instructional video, which he taught to a select group of older children. There were fifteen hundred children marching to the opening of the museum that day, which was something King had always endorsed: young people embracing the blues. For the children that day, it was a memorable introduction. B.B. King had demonstrated that it was okay for black people to embrace the blues and that the blues is just as significant as classical, jazz or any other musical artform.

14

NELLIE "MACK" McINNIS

Bass Player

The impact of music on Nellie McInnis has been holistic. It is her life and her livelihood. A consummate performer, Nellie looks forward to expressing herself musically, beyond fame and fortune. Nellie, who may be the only professional female bassist performing consistently in Mississippi, loves getting the gig, not so much for the money but for the practice and fellowship she has with other artists. Not a day goes by where she doesn't have a conversation with her bass instrument, which she affectionately calls "Thor."

Her brother, Walter Gardner, taught her to play the blues when she was young. Walter was an accomplished bassist who owned and operated Walter's School of Music in Jackson. Many bass players studied under his tutelage and have gone on to perform with major artists.

Nellie will tell you that she loves all genres of music, but gospel and blues have made the biggest impression on her because the songs are based on stories that are true for many people. Affectionately known as Nellie Mack, she grew up believing that B.B. King's name was B.B. *Kang* because that is how the folks in her neighborhood pronounced it. If music was heard coming from a neighbor's house, everyone would run to get a chair and gather around to listen. When B.B. King's music came over the airwaves, the neighbors would cry out, "That's B.B. *Kang*! That's B.B. *Kang*!"

Nellie thought she would become a professional tennis player until the day she stopped in on a band rehearsal at school. The director had stepped out for a moment, and Nellie joined the band by playing piano for them. Walking back in, the director found that everyone was having a good time. He told Nellie that there was an upcoming talent contest, and he wanted her to perform the song she had just been playing.

Nellie entered the contest and performed what she thought was just a little song. The school assembly loved it! The applause captivated her, and that was the beginning of her focus on music. She was fortunate to continue learning from her brother before he passed away, and she just couldn't get enough. Her upbringing taught her to respect master musicians, and she gravitated toward the music of B.B. King.

After dropping out of high school, Nellie began performing in bands, and they would often open shows with one of B.B. King's tunes. Eventually, she got her life on track and enrolled in college, continuing her music education while performing with musician friends and celebrities. Nellie graduated college with a bachelor's degree in music education; a master's degree in music education, specializing in strings; and a minor in psychology, reading and composition.

Nellie said, "Everybody has their own little spin on their musical abilities, but nobody plays like B.B. King." She continued, "We could play it close but not just like him." She was intrigued with how relaxed he was telling musical stories—each note of his instrumentation said something. Each note was filled with emotion.

In 2008, she was performing as part of King's opening act. After the performance, a man who was working with King's company managed to get her backstage to meet King. The man grabbed Nellie by the hand and said to her, "You ain't never met B.B., have you?"

She responded, "No, I've never met him."

"Well," the man said, "He has got to meet YOU!" When they arrived at King's dressing room, the man announced, "Look what I found."

King looked at her and said, "Another pretty lady?"

The man said, "She is pretty. But that ain't what I'm talking about. She plays bass."

King said, "Oh, really! Well, young lady, I'm looking forward to hearing you one day."

The man said, "B.B., you just heard her! That was her kicking it out there with that group."

King replied, "You're telling me this young lady was what I heard on that bass out there? Well, now. This is really something."

Sheepishly, Nellie responded, "I'm still learning."

B.B. pointed at her and said, "You keep that attitude right there. Don't ever let it go."

Nowadays, when Nellie talks about her musicality, she says, "I'm still under construction. I've got a long way to go."

King encouraged her by telling her that she should never feel like she's mastered the music. He said, "Just learn it each time you do it, and try to do it the best you can."

The next time Nellie met King was when she was scheduled to perform at one of his workshop presentations. She even had a chance to "hit a lick with him." He was teaching high school and college students at Mississippi Valley State University, and after the presentation, the participants had a chance to talk with him. Nellie sat in as if she were one of the students. When King looked out and saw her in the crowd, he said that the musicians should move out of the way so that the young people could learn. Nellie thought he was talking to someone behind her, so when the rest of the musicians moved away, she just stood there. "Would you please get on out of here?" he jovially asked her. Later, he chastised her and told her that she should have known better than to come in with the students, acting like she didn't know anything about music. "You've played with some of everybody. Let somebody else have a chance," he explained.

"What if I told you that I don't know what I'm doing?" Nellie was serious when she said that.

King told her, "Well, just keep doing whatever it is that you're doing."

In 2008, she performed for the grand opening of the B.B. King Museum. There were quite a few people on the set, and the musicians were relying on Nellie to hold the bass beats down. Afterward, King complimented her and said, "I get to hear you once again!"

Nellie shared what had become a joke between them, "I'm still learning!" She will always remember how he encouraged her.

He told her, "Never feel like you've mastered the music...just learn it each time you do it and try to do it the best you can."

In reflecting on the blues, Nellie noted that Muddy Waters, Howlin' Wolf, Son Thomas and Robert Johnson represent overlapping traditional music that evolved out of the Ma Rainey, Bessie Smith and Big Mama Thornton era. By the time B.B. King was laying down his patterns, he had a more exact sound that was opposed to the earlier blues sounds.

In counting the beats (one-two-three-four), the former musicians' one count was not always a one. Usually, every time you hit four, you go back to one, but in the early days, the one was not exact, especially in the music of Ma Rainey—one of the oldest examples of blues that can still be heard today. For B.B. King, that one was exact, with a sure-feeling groove behind it. B.B. King had a specific way of using his fingers on the frets, which some call trills, runs, shakes or slides. It's all about stamina and knowing what you want to achieve.

Nellie's advice to musicians is that they must love music and stay with it. It is important to make sure to find what you really love. Even if you don't want to perform as a musician, you can still be an enthusiast by learning everything you can about music—the ins and outs—and you can support musical endeavors. Or you can be a musicologist or ethnomusicologist and do research on music and music culture. There are so many different types of music careers, but you have to love music if you are going into any of those areas.

Hearing a great like B.B. King tell you to stay with it and stay on the right track is encouraging. The legendary Dizzy Gillespie once said, "Stay with it, and do your best. Do your homework. Eventually, you will come into your own style, and good things will happen, but there is no timeframe on when those things will happen for you." Similarly, Nellie tells upcoming artists to "find your higher power. Trust it to help you along the way." It is one of the components that has been most meaningful in her life.

Nellie Mack is a respected musician and a role model for young artists because she can share advice for living beyond music. Her advice to young artists is to use every experience to fill in the blanks of life because that is where the wisdom comes from. She tells young musicians,

> Once you learn how to do things through experience, you can then learn how to perform your music in peace. Every time you walk onto the stage, you should do so as if it is the first and/or the last time. You want to give all you can whether there are two people or two hundred thousand in the audience. Your music should not be anything less just because you don't see a whole lot of people sitting in the audience. Those few people in the audience came to see you. Always do your best whether you are in the classroom or elsewhere. Be professional.

One of the impressions B.B. King made on Nellie Mack was his attire and how important it was to his presentation. Today, her group decides together what they will wear on stage. Their outfits are often coordinated, and if there are both men and women on stage, they wear complimentary colors. Her bands have been known to have custom-made outfits, so their presentation will render a professional look.

Costume changes between sets were choreographed for musicians to keep the audience engaged. Nellie is a firm believer that African Americans should come with their best. Even back in the early days, performers dressed the part and were remembered for it. B.B. King always felt that this was important. King has been known to have said, "I grew up on the plantation in overalls. That's all I had to wear. I swore to God that if I lived to be a man, I would have other types of clothes to wear. I have a few pairs of jeans, but I don't wear them around the stage."

15

JESSE ROBINSON

Guitarist

Born in 1944 and raised in the Mississippi Delta, Jesse Robinson was the thirteenth of fourteen children. His father was a Pentecostal Holiness preacher, and his was a proud family. They never sharecropped—they worked their own plot of land.

Jesse's father and brother were musicians, and there was always a guitar around the house. Jesse learned to play from his brother, and the two would perform as backup behind their father in church. Jesse soon learned that gospel and blues are similar types of music, and the only thing that changes are the lyrics. The beats and the chord structure are the same.

The family moved to Jackson in 1960, where Jesse attended Brinkley High School. After graduating, he left Mississippi and was bound for Chicago. In 1962, when he was around eighteen years old, he had an opportunity to sit in with blues guitarist, singer and songwriter Elmore James, and he played with a lot of big bands during that time. In those days, you had to pay your dues, achieving a certain level of experience before performing on stage with professional musicians. "You had to be learned," Jesse said. "You had to know something." There were also some talented black musicians who were naturals. Jesse said that it came out of hard times for black men and their families. He also said that there was a time when everybody in his circle was playing blues and gospel. That's when he learned how to read music and make chord changes.

Robinson grew up listening to B.B. King. He said that King's music was so close to gospel that it would fit in with whatever style of life one had. Jesse never knew King to record an album that you couldn't sit down at the table with your family and listen to, which Robinson appreciated. Robinson said, "He kept it real." King was a product of the Holiness church from back in the day, and he stayed true to his roots. Many musicians step away from their origins to get famous and popular, but not King.

When Robinson moved back to Jackson in the 1980s, he was one of the opening acts for the Medgar Evers Homecoming event hosted by Charles Evers. While the band was on stage, Jesse had his eyes closed, as he always did while playing. He heard the people clapping, and he thought he had it going on, but when he opened his eyes, he saw that B.B. had come out of his dressing room and was standing by the stage watching the band. Jesse had met some of the other well-known musicians during his time on the road with Little Milton, another band member, but he had not had a chance to meet B.B. yet. Whenever the King was around, you always had to stand in line to talk to him. The homecoming was how Jesse first met B.B. King. After that encounter, B.B. would always invite Jesse up on the stage to perform with him and to be a part of whatever he was doing.

Jesse was on the advisory board for the B.B. King Museum. During the opening concert, Jesse was out in the audience taking pictures when B.B. quieted the band and pointed Jesse out to the crowd, telling everyone who he was. Jesse said, "He boosted me up real good! I only had twenty dollars in my pocket, but he made me feel like a millionaire." Then King invited him to come up on stage and play. Without his guitar, Jesse wasn't prepared, but King didn't miss a beat. He asked his own guitarist to lend Jesse his instrument. Jesse has been fortunate to have such interactions with King on more than one occasion. He even presented annual workshops with King for several years at Mississippi Valley State University.

One day while B.B. King was being interviewed by a newspaper and Jesse was standing nearby, King stopped the interview and said, "There's the gentleman y'all need to be interviewing: Mr. Jesse Robinson from Jackson, Mississippi! Come on up here with me, Jesse."

Jesse laughed while telling this story and said, "He would always make me nervous."

Jesse Robinson said, "B.B. King is one of the most popular men on the face of God's earth because everybody wants to play Lucille. They want to play, sing and be like B.B. There is no one else with that popularity." Indeed, when Jesse was on the board for the museum, the FBI had to do a background check on King before they would put his name on the museum. They couldn't find one flaw on the King: no drunk driving, no abuse, no

B.B. King Museum in Indianola, Mississippi. *Courtesy of Susan Liles.*

drugs, no jail record, nothing. The only issue they found was that he had gotten in trouble with the IRS in the mid-'60s, but he straightened that out. There was also one time when he was trying to get back to Memphis on Highway 61 when the police pulled him over and put him in jail all night long. They couldn't find anything else.

That said, B.B. King was a self-professed womanizer and enjoyed the company of beautiful women. When asked about the fourteen or fifteen children King had, Jesse refused to comment. He responded with what he knew about King: "He was all about cheering people up. He never tried to be disrespectful." Right now, Jesse said that we are at a great loss with King's passing. There are no other musicians out there with his status because B.B. was so correct and professional. He had to be a God-sent man to have played for kings, queens and presidents. He played for everyone.

Jesse said that blues music came from a cultural struggle:

> *Don't forget! Just because we used the term slavery that it is all over now. It's not over. If you look at it today, it still means the same thing. It comes from a struggle. There was racism, and there is still racism. If we talk about it, we have a better chance of doing something about it. There was a time when blacks couldn't go to a white restaurant; we couldn't ride on the front of the bus; we were mistreated in all forms, fashions and ways; and*

people would make up songs, harmonizing songs: "I'm gonna catch the first thing smoking. I'm going to leave this old town." That's a communication. The singer is telling people that he is going to leave and, one morning, you wake up and he's gone. Black people sing songs now about their problems. If you've got a problem and things are not working out for you and you're being pushed back, well, remember the saying, "If you're black, get back. If you're brown, stick around. If you're white, you're right." It is still that same way. Things are a lot better than they used to be for blacks. But it is not over. We have a long way to go. We have not hit the halfway mark yet. And that is where blues music comes from. People would just make up stuff to express what they were going through, and it was written as twelve bars, and chord changes were made on every fourth of the twelfth bar, then it would repeat back to the beginning. That's the basic format, twelve-bar blues. There is also sixteen-bar blues, twenty-four-bar blues. But twelve-bar blues was the basic format back in the day. You can rhyme it with a catch, but some people don't feel the need to rhyme when their lyrics are strong enough. The blues was a lot of repeating back in the day and that would really get in your head. If you say it one time and move on, the listener might miss it, but if you repeat it, it begins to register.

Jesse Robinson throws himself a birthday party every year. He said, "If I don't do it, who will?" The event, which is open to the public, includes a strong lineup of blues musicians. He's been doing it for almost fifty years. The party is not all about him, since the events are usually standing room only. For Robinson, it is about the people and the musicians coming together. It is a statement to the community to keep the music alive, and it just happens to take place on his birthday. Jesse supports the creative economy by bringing together so many musicians, saying that "People who need people are the luckiest people in the world." Finally, Jesse said that when you humble yourself, you have a chance to learn, a chance to pass things on and a chance for fellowship. You have a chance to build friendships and communications, social media and the whole bit.

Jesse Robinson's music is as recognizable as B.B. King's. You can walk into a venue and recognize his style before even seeing him. Jesse will tell you that "it is a recipe, a signature." He wasn't trying to do that at first, but it has come out in the way he puts it all together. He agrees that B.B. had a distinctive style: "When a musician plays like that, they can excel. It's a language and when you speak it well, people don't forget." After the death of B.B. King, Jesse Robinson was honored with an opportunity to tour with King's band.

16

MELVIN HENDREX

"House Cat"

MELVIN L. Hendrex Jr. is known to both friends and acquaintances as "House Cat." He was given the name because of an incident that took place when he was three years old. He would often sleep by the fireplace on the floor of the living room late at night while his grandfather, Bud, played poker with friends in the dining room. The fireplace could be seen from both sides of the wall that adjoined the two rooms, and Bud and his friends were able to see the sleeping boy through the fire's glow. Bud had been on a winning streak for a while, but one night he was losing. Bud's friends said that he was losing because the black cat lying on the rug on the other side of the fireplace was bringing him bad luck. That's how Melvin got his nickname.

House Cat would get spankings when he didn't respond whenever his mother called him by his nickname. He hated the name. Things changed a few years later when a girl he had a crush on heard someone call out to him, and it finally became his stage name years later when blues musician Albert King heard about him.

House Cat's music is a collaboration of everything he has gone through in more than seventy years of life. He was a voice major and piano minor in college, and very few people know that he worked with an opera guild. He didn't like wearing the "I Dream of Genie" outfits back then because men were tagged as being soft and girly if they performed in operas. During the early days of his career, he had to perform a lot of songs that he didn't like. He studied under Emma Golden while in elementary school and college.

She helped him find his sound rather than just select the music he liked. She helped him with his tone and breathing. He learned jazz, but he was not able to make a living with jazz. His music is a collaboration of jazz, blues and gospel, and you can hear all the under- and overtones from each genre when he performs.

House Cat is the brother of R & B singer Dorothy Moore. Moore is best known for her 1976 hit "Misty Blue." The song is still heard on the radio and on movie soundtracks. Their father, Melvin Hendrex, performed under the name "Melvin Henderson." He was a member of the Five Blind Boys of Mississippi.

At one of the B.B. King Homecoming events, House Cat noticed something amiss. Just before his gig with his sister, he saw that the stage lighting was terrible because 15,000-watt canisters were being used. The computer screen on his keyboard caught a terrible glare from the lights, and he couldn't see it very well. When Dorothy sang that night, House Cat was not able to cue the keyboard, and he gave what he feels was the worst performance of his career.

Embarrassed after the show, House Cat backed his wheelchair over to the bus stop. B.B. King walked over and saw the wheelchair and asked someone to bring him a chair so he could sit down next to the musician and talk. House Cat remembered that King spoke to him on a human level. He let him know that it was all right and that things often get better. He talked to House Cat about musicians he had studied as a young boy and about some of the ideas he got from other people. House Cat recalled that King was a very giving person who freely shared what he knew.

As a young musician during the '70s and early '80s, House Cat remembers listening to musicians talk backstage. He's heard many musicians tell stories over the years—Albert King, Tyrone Davis, Little Milton, Z.Z. Hill and B.B. King were all storytellers. They would jokingly share experiences. House Cat remembers overhearing a story about the time King stopped in on one of Z.Z. Hill's gigs to check on him, only to find out that Hill didn't have enough money to pay the band. The producer ran out before paying the band. B.B. King took care of making sure that Hill's band members got paid. In hindsight, they laughed about it. House Cat said that musicians would look out for each other like that.

King used to tell stories about being on the road. He talked about how musicians would be piled together in one car and how it would take hours to get from New York to somewhere like Virginia. After long hours on the road and then the gig, promoters would often go out the back door with the money and leave the musicians hanging. As a result, King would try to get his money from the promoters before the performance.

House Cat recalled that during the early days when B.B. King recorded in the studio, only one song could be recorded at a time. If someone made a mistake, they would have to go back to the beginning and start over again. They had to get one song perfect before they could move on to the next, and it could take a month or more before they got the whole album down. Now it only takes a few days: individual artists can lay fifteen to twenty tracks and then edit and clean it up. As House Cat said, "The cake was good and the icing great, but the icing ain't nothing without the cake."

House Cat said that King's sound changed tremendously, noting that "The Thrill Is Gone" is related to the old jubilee sound. He feels that the fans from the early days never got used to the new music King was creating. He thinks it is ironic that King's fans didn't get into his work with Eric Clapton—the old listeners don't like the new sound, and the new listeners don't like the old sound.

Before gospel music, there was jubilee music. You could hear jubilee sounds coming out of the cotton fields in the early blues days. Today, the music is a derivative of those early ideas. On the other hand, quartet singing had a different feel. You couldn't just sit there and listen to it. As a boy coming up in the church, B.B. experienced old men tapping their toes (heel/toe), which would give him the feel for what the bass drum and snare drum would do in a musical interaction. Sometimes there would be a piano, never strings, but you had "that feel." Musicians today call it "that pocket." When House Cat played drums years ago, his instructors taught him to make the instrument sound like a variety of sounds. Now you can hear each instrument individually and collectively.

King always had rhythm, and you can hear his patterns all the way through his songs. His guitar was always singing a little line throughout the song and was never interrupted by the playing of chords. Playing chords while singing is like dividing the brain into four sections. Drummers do it well: they can have one pattern going with their right foot and another pattern going with their left foot, while their hands do something that solidifies the rhythm. King, however, played licks between a lyric. He sang a line then played a line, all within one phrase. He had a rhythm guitarist playing the chords for him.

House Cat considers himself a "jitterbug" who rose behind most of the master musicians he hung out with over the years. The way King carried himself professionally was passed down to musicians like him. There is a pride that drives many of the musicians to mentor one another, but King always paved the way. House Cat ended his reflections by recalling a quote from Dorothy Norwood of the Gospel Caravans, who spoke about musicians expressing life through song: "We don't look like where we've been, and we don't look like what we've been through."

17

BEN PAYTON

Blues Guitarist and Singer

A blues historian, storyteller and musician (singer/guitarist), Ben Payton's roots run deep in the soil of Mississippi. In 1964, he left the state as a teenager and headed to Chicago. He returned to Mississippi as a professional musician in 2003.

After a year or so in Chicago, he met some doo-wop singers. In the 1940s through the 1960s, doo-wop singing was trendy among African American and Italian American teenagers who had a talent for making harmonies. They would stand outside storefronts, on corners, in subway stations or anywhere they could captivate an audience with their a cappella phrasing of the latest R & B songs. According to Payton, this style of singing was mostly popular in northern cities and in California.

A friend told Ben that a group was looking for a bass singer, and he said he would give it a try. Like many of the guys who stood on corners singing the harmonies of the day, this group sang to attract female attention. They drank wine and expressed themselves without any thought of becoming professional musicians.

At that time, Ben wasn't really into singing, but music stimulated the memory of something that had happened earlier in his life. When he was seven or eight, he heard his first marching band play, and it caught his attention. He left school energized, went home and found a ten-gallon lard can. He crafted two sticks and tried to mimic the sound he had heard earlier in the day. He beat on the can until he busted it, and not long after that, his mother purchased a cheap guitar for him to play. Unfortunately, he left it outside where it was ruined by rain.

When Ben left the doo-wop group, he bought himself a Silvertone guitar and amplifier. He purchased the guitar from the Sears, Roebuck and Company department store on time (on credit). He didn't know how to play it, but the Silvertone guitars were easy to tune. Sears made inexpensive guitars that came with instructions on how to tune them—you didn't have to know much about guitars to know how to play it with that type of tuning. At the age of sixteen or seventeen, Ben started playing the guitar without direction and began singing with a group of young musicians. The blues did not enter Ben's world again until he was older. He decided that he had no more desire to play in a group and determined that he wanted to be more intimate with the audience, so he tried folk music. But what he really needed to do was make some money, and performing folk music was not going to help him do that.

In 1975, Ben performed with the Howlin' Wolf Band. Howlin' Wolf was already deceased at the time, but the band continued to perform. A street musician came from New York to hear the band, and he had a '78 album of Robert Johnson's music with him. Ben had an opportunity to meet the guy, and it was the first time he had heard Robert Johnson's music. He knew about the blues because he had heard other musicians, but it just hadn't been his thing.

When he heard Johnson's record, he couldn't believe that he was hearing one guitar play with such diversity. Payton was fascinated that one guitar player could play all of the parts simultaneously. Johnson had a style like folk music, where the thumb is doing one thing, the fingers are doing another, and the left hand is doing something different. Ben described it as a sort of "dupe de dupe de jing ing jing ing" and "dupe de dupe de," all at the same time. It is like both sides of the brain are working to capture what is going on in the left and right hands. Ben's style was to play a chord and make chord changes, then put a little melody into it. He found the experience exhilarating.

In 1972, after returning from North Africa, Ben ran into Artie "Blues Boy" White, who was opening for B.B. King at the High Chaparral in Chicago. Two nights before the gig, during rehearsal, Payton needed to make notations to the songs, but all he had was a piece of yellow paper. Artie gave him a red ink pen, and Payton wrote down the references. On the night of the performance, the group went out onto the stage. The technicians turned on the red and yellow lights, and when Ben looked at the paper, the colored lights made it look blank. He couldn't see a thing, nor could he remember the music. Artie started cussing. Ben asked him to just tell the band what key he was going to sing in, but Artie didn't know. He made something up, and when the band started playing in that key, it was too high for Artie's vocal range. The performance was ruined.

When it was over, Ben went upstairs and found that B.B. King was sitting in the vestibule. B.B. said, "Man, I heard y'all out there, and you sounded good." But Ben knew that it was one of the worst nights he had ever had on stage. King knew what he had been through, and he was trying to offer encouragement.

From that time on, Ben really focused on blues music. He always knew that B.B. and Albert King received a lot of attention, but he didn't have enough experience to know about their skills. He was older and had time to explore the differences in the two Kings' styles. He came to realize something: each of their styles built up from the heart. B.B.'s guitar talks, and his music tells a story, and Albert talks and sings like a preacher. Albert's real last name was Nelson, but he changed it to King. Some people thought he might have been B.B. King's brother, and that very well may have been his intention. If that was his purpose, there was really no need. He was a good singer and an incredible guitarist.

In a recent conversation, Payton reflected on how the music of black people has evolved. He said that the first note of the blues was played on the water—on the boat from Africa to America. He went on to observe:

> this music was voiced in the notes sung in the holding pen before the Africans got on the boat. You can imagine the sounds in the hearts of people that had been stolen away from their culture, away from their communities, placed on a big ship on the largest expanse of water they had ever seen. Packed tightly together on the boat, they were separated from friends and family and placed in different culture groups. They communicated through humming and moaning, vocalizations that expressed their plight. Once they reached land in America and were sold at market, their expressions told their stories in emotional chords and rhythms. What better way to deal with life's misfortune, than to pour sorrow and suffering into songs? When a slave would get whipped, they would try to comfort one another. In comforting one another, that's where the sound began to be more expressive, a sound they took to the [cotton] fields.

For these individuals, the moan songs became their way of thinking out loud. They would moan to signify, "How am I ever going to get back home?" They couldn't say anything about this out loud, but those same emotions ended up in the church. That's where many of those field songs are now, songs like, "I Love the Lord; He Heard My Cry." They called the author of that song Dr. Watts, but it was the representation of field songs.

Over time, African Americans found their voices and began to compose lyrics of their own. During the latter part of the nineteenth century and the early twentieth century, they would sing about anything and everything. Banjo and fiddle were the main instruments, but they were hard to come by. Musicians used spoons and washboards, and they would even beat on tables.

At the turn of the twentieth century, the mood of gospel could be heard in songs the community played during parties. They wanted to have songs for the parties, so that is when they started the revelry—the barn and corn songs, such as "I was with my baby last night, I held her," reminiscent of Paul Laurence Dunbar's "When Malindy Sings." When the era arrived in which banjos and guitars were more readily available—the late 1910s—musicians created songs for every occasion. Prior to that, guitars, which originated in Spain and gravitated to America in the sixteenth century, were so expensive that slaves or, later in history, former slaves couldn't afford to buy them.

When Negro minstrel shows came on the scene, women performers joined men on stage. Some say blues music was started by women like Gertrude "Ma" Rainey (1886–1939), affectionately known as the Mother of the Blues, and Bessie Smith, affectionately called the Empress of the Blues. Indeed, some even say that Rainey coined the term *blues*, but the truth is probably more complex. The term may have been heard in another region prior to Ma Rainey.

Regarding the origin of the minstrel shows, Payton said that they were preceded by the more common medicine doctor shows where snake oils and tonics were sold by traveling salesmen. The word *minstrel* is a spinoff of the word *medicine*, and these shows were forerunners to vaudeville shows. When the minstrel shows came to town, it was a time for the community to come together. Tents would be set up along the waterfront towns and there would be all kinds of performances. Prior to emancipation, minstrel shows were performed by whites who would make fun of black people. After emancipation, performances usually took place at the barn or at the house. These were the only stages available for blacks before minstrel shows came to town. The most famous of the minstrel shows that showcased black performers was the Rabbit's Foot Company.

When slavery ended in the mid-1860s, blacks began to express themselves more freely. You can just imagine that, although times were still hard, blacks had some joy to sing about, and they could begin to express themselves as they gathered from house to house. They began to express different things, composing songs about what they knew or what they were going through during the day—now that they didn't have to work for "Old Massa" anymore. They started singing songs with lines like "old Master buy a brand-new coat and hang it on the wall. Darkie take that same old coat and wear it to the ball" and "old Master riding on his horse and fell off." According to Payton, songs like these are also part of the origin of the blues.

What are the blues of old? The suffering of the Negro—a person who is captured against his will and made to work for no money, and he can't do anything about it; a person locked up within himself; a person whose lack of freedom takes away his ability to control his own actions. That is the blues. A person whose freewill has been taken away has no will. That was the blues from a long time ago.

The blues is also when a man talks about a rough time he has had with his woman. Now, this is no different from what any other race goes through. Every race of men has problems with their women, and everybody has experienced hard times. But not everyone has had their freewill snatched up from under them, and they couldn't do anything about it. That's the blues black folks were living. It was just sung to a different tune.

It is important to learn about the foundation of music. The plantation owners' children had instruments. Black folks would hear them playing those instruments, and they wanted to learn how to play. Oftentimes, slaves didn't have instruments, but instead used sticks, cans and their bodies to play music called "hambone," by hitting one's arms, chest, legs, jaws, etc. According to Payton, much of the original blues music can be divided into four areas: Appalachia, New York and New England states are in the Eastern area; Minnesota to Oregon is the Northwestern area; Texas to California represents the Southwestern area; and finally, the Southeast is composed of the Mississippi, Georgia, Alabama and Florida region. When slaves first came to America, they arrived in the Appalachian area—in Virginia and the Carolinas—on slave ships. This is where it all started because many other areas had not even been settled.

A lot happened along the Ohio and Mississippi Rivers. Those were the trade routes from Minnesota to New Orleans and from New York to Texas. Then there was land travel. Music was influenced by Italians and Germans, among others. This is where the coal mine and railroad fellows learned to play music and influenced others. People think blues started in Mississippi, and we have heard the saying that Mississippi is the root of American music. But every state uses some aspect of "this is where it started." There is some truth in the saying because a certain style of music did start in Mississippi. The Delta blues has its own personality, and the same is true with the Black Hill Country blues. The music of gandy dancers originated with railroad workers and prisoners toiling in work camps—it was a different sound than the songs of the cotton fields. There was not a lot of danger found working in the cotton fields, but the songs of workers in the prison and rail camps had to be more precise to avoid injury. Every time the men grunted, "Hawh!" you had to get your feet out of the way. It was the same way with men and power: one man couldn't move a train track by himself, but when the men worked together and sang a shout, they could move whole rails. When the men grunted out loud, they made an incredible sound. It was a music unto its own era that didn't carry over to any other.

Payton reflected on when he was a small boy of five years old playing ball outside. A neighbor yelled and told him to stop playing ball, saying that it was the devil's game. Young Payton couldn't understand why the neighbor was saying something like that, and her comments stuck with him all his life. She didn't know you could have fun, enjoy life and be a person of faith. Even today, when you go to church, the only reason they say that the blues is the devil's music is because it doesn't say, "Thank you, Lord." Yet, if you read the scriptures, God talks about expressing life, such as when God says, "When Israel was young, I loved him, now Israel has turned its back on me." Isn't that the same as saying, "Baby, when I met you, you were sweet sixteen; but now you done run away from me"? A lot of people couldn't read in the early days of the blues, so they were not able to parallel oral tradition with written scripture.

If you ever have a chance to talk with Ben Peyton, you will find that when it comes to music, he is a philosopher. In 2011, Peyton represented Mississippi in Washington, D.C., for the American Folklife Center's Homegrown Concert Series presented by the Library of Congress.

18

DEXTER ALLEN

Let it Lead You

D exter Allen was born and raised in Crystal Springs, Mississippi. He has been around the blues all his life. He has lived the blues, experienced the blues and now he sings the blues. If you ask Dexter what the blues is all about, he will respond with a story. Dexter will tell you that the blues represents a certain culture, particularly the experience of African Americans in times past. For him, musicians such as Muddy Waters, Robert Johnson, Howlin' Wolf and B.B. King were the pioneers. They set the trend and were the cornerstones that you could see and hear. Their songs spoke to the culture and struggle from which the music came.

In describing people's relationship with the blues, Dexter said that sometimes it is hard to understand its history or significance if you have not been around it. Other cultures can provide insight on this point, such as Chinese and Japanese societies whose heritage is rooted in a culture that has stood the test of time. Just like for them, martial arts are considered entertainment, we look at the blues as entertainment.

Dexter considers himself an aspiring blues artist who tells young people to embrace the blues. He said, "Let it meet you. Respect where it came from but create it in today's terms so that it can be accepted." According to Dexter, there are three key elements of any successful blues song: (1) story, (2) emotion and (3) delivery. Blues pioneers of old spoke about trials they experienced and things they saw, in life, in culture and in society. He said he will never experience going out into the fields to pick cotton or walking up Highway 61 with his guitar on his back or singing from shack to shack. He won't experience that because he has too many vehicles and he doesn't have to walk anywhere. He said he is not going to pick cotton, but he can buy things that are made with cotton. It is a different day and era now. Sometimes the blues historian will look at the younger artists of today and say, "Well, that ain't blues. You're not traditional enough."

To this point, Dexter was passionate in saying that a Chevrolet today is not going to look like it did back in 1957. Everything has evolved. We have evolved, so we must embrace the music and the culture. But out of all the music festivals in the world, there are more blues festivals in the world than any other genre of music because of how the music speaks to us.

The Rolling Stones were interested in coming to the United States partially due to the fact that they liked the way American blues music sounded. It was the emotion that went into it—the struggle. The Rolling Stones did not understand it, but when they heard it, they could feel it: "Oh, baby, you don't have to go." When you heard someone sing that type of song, you got a sense that the singer was pouring out his or her heart. The emotion captivated us then and still endears us to the blues today. When you can write about your blues of today, then you can capture the environment of your story because maybe you lived it, and even if you haven't lived it, you can relate to it, because it is something relative to today's era.

That's one of Dexter's platforms in bridging the younger generation to the root of where the blues came from. Mainstream media has made it so that when you see blues on television, you see something that is old school. You won't see blues artists on MTV. The mainstream media has not encouraged younger generations to want to embrace the blues because it looks dated when you see it. Maybe it is the image of a guy in his sixties or seventies with his guitar and a hat that is the media's view of the origin of the blues, but that's the blues of yesterday. Dexter said that he doesn't sit on a porch with a straw hat on his head and a toothpick hanging from his mouth: "That's not the blues musician of today. We have to make it attractive!"

Dexter's records captivate today's listeners because when you hear them, you can't automatically put them into a category. But for all intents and purposes, he calls it the blues. He wants young people to hear his music and say, "Man, I didn't know that blues sounded like that!" He encourages young people to embrace what the blues once was, but then reach out to the artists of today who have embodied the blues. He considers himself a blues soul artist just like other musicians call themselves blues rock artists—they

(Left to right) Angela Dupard, Dexter Allen and Kristen Dupard. *Courtesy of Susan Liles.*

are bringing in modern elements, but the foundation of their music is still the blues. As innovative as Muddy Waters and Howlin' Wolf were prior to the 1970s, you can be assured that if they were here today, they would not sound like they did back in 1955 because they would have continued to evolve. Dexter noted that B.B. King has opened many doors and cleared the way for a lot of people.

Dexter advises anyone who wants to develop an affection for the blues to "Let it lead you—don't try to grab it and make it what you want it to be—it is already well represented. It is not a black or white thing; it represents a culture and a way of life. It also represents an era in time." A lot of the songs sung prior to emancipation were just a way to communicate from person to person and from plantation to plantation. Today, the blues represents a distinct way of life, just like it did at the turn of the twentieth century. But the times are not the same. Now you can apply the blues to your livelihood, what you're living and what you're seeing.

In Dexter's Blues in Schools workshop, he wrote a song called "Math Test Blues." The song references a kid who played around all evening when he should have been studying for a math test. The next morning, he found himself sitting in his math class feeling the blues because he wasn't prepared for the test.

What are your blues of today? Many people have the blues. Imagine seeing a child trying to unwrap the packaging from a piece of candy, and he just can't get it open. He's catching the blues. Dexter said,

> *Make it relevant. The blues ain't always a sad thing. When the singer croons "My dog left me," or "My wife ran off with the preacher," that's the blues for sure, but in times gone by, it also represented struggle. It was a release to go off to the juke joints and sing, "Oh, Mr. Charlie, your windmill burning down; big boss man, can you hear me when I call." Blues musicians of old could only sing about what they had experienced.*

As a musician, Dexter learned early on to quench the anger he felt about the lack of blacks attending blues events across the diaspora. They just weren't filling the seats. He thought that black people would love the blues at those festivals, especially traditional blues festivals, but they just weren't showing up. He asked, "Where are my people? I don't see them!" He started asking people why they didn't like the blues. The average younger African American, between the ages of thirteen and twenty-five, would respond, "I don't really listen to the blues." Dexter had to realize that to the people for whom the struggle was created, the blues was a part of their ancestry. It is a part of their life story, their reality. Either we have lived it ourselves, or we knew somebody—grandmama, grand-uncle or somebody else—who went through that struggle. It is either a reality to us, or, for those who haven't experienced it, it is entertainment. Oftentimes, we don't want to hear blues music because it reminds us of struggle. But in general, the young people of today don't know anything about it. When granddaddy talks about how he used to work for a dollar a day, you can put jazz, country and hip-hop together, and you ask a young person to relate this topic to a genre of music, they will select the blues.

"Coming Home to Mississippi" is Dexter's song about how he was raised, but he wants the message to get out that "Mississippi ain't like it used to be." Every state, every town and every city has its own history, and anywhere in the South can attest to having dirt behind its ears. But it is not that way today. Dexter wants to paint a picture that makes people realize that Mississippi is okay. He wants people to know that he loves Mississippi, and he would never live anywhere else. Does Mississippi love him? He doesn't know. He can't live his life wondering about that. He must do what he can to leave his legacy for someone else to follow.

The people who attended B.B. King's concerts were true to him because he stayed true to them. They understood the struggle, they understood what it represented, and they will always honor that. Dexter is serious when he says, "If I live to be ninety-five, and I can't do what I used to do, I believe there will be people that will respect what the music represented throughout my life and they will always honor what I've done to keep the blues alive."

19

ROBERT HILL

Owner, Radio Station WRNE 980 FM, Pensacola, Florida

R obert Hill is from Montgomery, Alabama. He is one of the last black broadcasters. He has been blazing a trail as a disc jockey since 1969. Hill will tell you that he is "just making a living and enjoying life," and there is nothing he likes better than the blues. He thanks his father for introducing him to blues music.

Hill has been fortunate in his long broadcasting career to observe people who love blues music, and he said they are some of the best people he has ever known. He referenced the likes of Little Milton, Z.Z. Hill and many others. He called them great humanitarians and said, "There is something magical about how blues musicians have mentored one another and worked together."

Hill went through a lot of ridicule about playing the blues on his radio station, WRNE, in Pensacola, Florida. Staunch Christians have spoken out against his station's all-day blues programming. When asked what changes he is seeing from twentieth- to twenty-first-century blues, Hill said that there are some people who want to change the name of blues to Southern soul. Hill said that Southern soul is good, but the name shouldn't change from the blues. Southern soul is an extension of the blues. Blues has found its traditional home base in the Delta, St. Louis, Chicago and Texas. He suggested that we should not change the name of the blues just because we think it is depressing. There are a lot of young musicians on the horizon who are looking at new genres of the blues, but who may not necessarily want to hold on to blues traditions. According to Hill, B.B. King contributed so much to the blues, defining and redefining the music and capturing the foundation of the music.

What is the origin of blues music? He said that some say that it began in Africa with the griots. As they migrated to other parts of the world, the root and rhythms arrived in Mexico, Australia, Hong Kong and Hungary. Wherever blacks were imported throughout the diaspora, that culture has been impacted by the influence of the rhythms. W.C. Handy said that it evolved in the Southern plantation fields because the blacks who were held in captivity were from different tribes and, at first, didn't speak the same language. They were creative in their ability to communicate by humming and moaning. That was the origin of blues music.

Mississippi is a magical state. According to Hill, so many individuals who have become something musically were either born in the state or have some type of ancestral link to the state.

Hill posed a rhetorical question: "What else can we do to expose our people to the blues?" He said that he has been trying to encourage everybody out there—the Billy "Soul" Bonds, the Milton Campbells, the Willie Claytons and others. He encourages them to write, even if they just start writing about what happens on the road. It would be an invitation for others to read and learn about blues musicians. He also encourages blues musicians to learn something about the musicians who went before them because they are standing on their proverbial shoulders.

As a younger man, Hill traveled along the Chitlin' Circuit. Robert Hill said that he encourages musicians to write about it and capture anecdotes from that time. He believes that people would love to read about the documentation and history of the blues from that perspective.

Robert Johnson, Charley Patton, Son House—those guys laid down the foundation of the blues that has been copied over and over. Hill said that we must focus on the blues musicians of today as well as the blues musicians of old. B.B. King was one of the greats, one of the most well-known and respected blues musicians of all time. In Hill's words, "We can't disown any part of the blues because it is part of our heritage."

20

JaWONN SMITH

Southern Soul

When JaWonn Smith's single "I Got This Record" was released, it was very popular on the R & B charts and received a lot of radio play. WRNE in Pensacola played it constantly, as did other stations throughout the region. JaWonn's style of blues is called Southern soul. According to JaWonn, his music is a true mix of rhythm and blues. Growing up, he listened to the blues because that's what his mother listened to on the radio. He was too young to voice an opinion about what he wanted to hear. So, he grew up listening to soul singer Tyrone Davis, blues singer B.B. King and Johnny Taylor, who sang multiple genres of music.

As his voice matured, he began to sing in church. Folks kept telling him that he had a soulful voice, not a gospel voice. JaWonn began writing in his journal about whatever was going on in his life. He didn't have a rough life, but neither was it an easy, peaches-and-cream existence. When he became a professional singer, his manager told him that he was a storywriter. JaWonn is young, but he recognizes that B.B. King was one of the best storywriters. "That's really what the blues is all about," he said. "Blues tells you a story. It can put you in sync with what you've been feeling. It represents true living."

He comes to the blues with an understanding of his culture and feels that he is a face that young people can relate to. When audiences see JaWonn, they are often surprised because they thought he was much older than his mid-twenties, given his style of singing. The youth, however, recognize him right away because of his presence on the radio and in social networks. They have fallen in love with his music, and his career is on track.

JaWonn was not surprised that his career took off so fast, humbly stating that he has always had a relationship with God. He didn't know the day or time, but he knew it was going to happen. He felt that it was just like anything else. Keep working hard at it and eventually it will take off is his motto. He is surprised by the age range of the people singing his songs. From two to sixty-two, people are singing his songs and professing that he is a soulful singer. JaWonn appreciates his fans and said, "Without the people, I'm nobody!"

JaWonn feels that B.B. King was the "number one guy of the blues." He thinks that there is no one above King. He looks to Bobby Rush, too, then Mel Waiters, T.K. Soul and Sir Charles Jones. He is one of the first to tell you that right now, many people know B.B. King as the face of the blues. JaWonn said that if he gets a chance to make it to King's level, he believes that many more young people will accept the blues. He said that King left us a legacy. He can't say what his own legacy will be, but he feels that he will bring this new genre of music, Southern soul, to the world. He thinks that his music is a strong mixture of new age blues and R & B. He wants to encourage young people and said, "You don't have to take your clothes off. You can get up on the stage without gimmicks, and people will respect you for it." Nowadays, many of the youth think that they want to be rappers—they think that they must dance around on stage to get attention. Smith believes you can get up on the stage and just flat-out sing and make it.

On stage, JaWonn is charismatic. He almost doesn't even have to sing. The audiences love him so much that after he pours his heart into a few bars from his lyrics, he just turns the microphone toward the audience, and they start singing the rest of his song for him. His song "I've Got This Record" received a lot of attention on the radio. In response, he said, "That is nothing but God!" The song has played on the airwaves in places that have taken JaWonn by surprise, and now he says he is trying to catch up with the success of his music. He is thankful he knew B.B. King's music while King was alive. You never want a legend to leave this world, but he looks at King and wonders what if someone like Sam Cooke had lived as long. King had an opportunity to do so much and encourage so many. JaWonn is thankful that the King left so much and that so many can learn from his legacy.

21

ABDUL RASHEED

Singer and Bass Player

Abdul Rasheed met B.B. King in the 1950s, when he was thirteen years old and working at the Heidelberg Hotel in Greenwood, Mississippi. He got the job when he lied about his age and told the hotel management that he was eighteen when, in fact, he was only twelve. The men who worked with him thought he was eighteen as well.

One night, they went out to Willie Stevenson's Rose Bowl in Jackson, where B.B. King was playing. Rasheed liked Sam Cooke, but he was impressed with the way King performed. Rasheed has been singing all his life and taught himself to play guitar when he was eighteen. At the time of this interview, Rasheed was seventy-three. He has experienced everything from hard rock to the Motown sound and has performed on many continents. But he didn't get into the blues until he heard "The Thrill Is Gone." Rasheed is a bass player, and the beat in that song really got to him, as did B.B.'s song "Why I Sing the Blues." At that point, he started studying "good" blues. Some people told him that blues music was depressing. Then Muddy Waters came out with a song that said, "The blues had a baby, and they named it rock and roll." Rasheed went on to say that "the blues had a baby and they called it country and western. The blues had a baby and they named it hillbilly." It all came from the blues and "this man B.B. King was doing it." Rasheed recalled that B.B. King and Bobby "Blue" Bland "told a heck of a story."

One day Rasheed was performing at a park on Highway 49. B.B. King was on the same program. Rasheed's children, who were very small at the time, were in attendance, and they went back to meet B.B. King after the performance. King asked Rasheed who he had with him, and Rasheed introduced his family. King held the baby girl in his arms and said, "I'm glad that you brought her. A lot of men don't hang out with their children like that." He said, "I'm glad you brought her to the concert. Our people are basically getting rid of the blues, but this is something that we need to continue with our children because it is God's gift."

Rasheed's baby daughter attended daycare, and her teacher was a B.B. King fanatic. The teacher called Rasheed and asked him to come to the school to discuss his daughter's behavior. She told him that she wanted her children to have imagination, but that his daughter's imagination was incredible. Rasheed asked for further explanation, and the teacher said that his daughter told the class that her father took her to a B.B. King concert and that King held her and kissed her on her hand. Rasheed explained that his daughter told the truth—it really happened.

Rasheed has had opportunities to be on stage with B.B. King, Kris Kristofferson and others in Fayette, Mississippi. Sometimes they would have a jam session after the performance, and King would invite the musicians to come up and perform on stage. He would even let some of the up-and-coming musicians play his guitar, but being a bass player, Rasheed never had a chance to play Lucille.

Rasheed's aunt Mattie Pace Scott called B.B. King "Riley." She was his babysitter on the plantation where King's parents worked when he was a small boy. She wasn't much older than King, but it was customary for the older children to help take care of the smaller ones. She was 16 when B.B. was just a small child. As an adult, Aunt Mattie went on to have nine children of her own, six of whom have doctoral degrees. She was very bright and had a great memory, and even at 102, you couldn't beat her playing checkers and other games. She passed away in 2013.

B.B. King played at the Magnolia Club in Indianola years ago, and Rasheed had an opportunity to be there and performed as well. The two talked and had a good time. Rasheed described King as "a magnificent person." He always had a smile and a good word for you. In 2014, Rasheed could tell that King was getting older. Rasheed said that King has done a lot for black people—he was a great ambassador for the blues.

Today, Rasheed is the talent coordinator for the Central Mississippi Blues Society. The Central Mississippi Blues Society band is a smorgasbord of musicians who have performed with singers such as Latimore. The group that Rasheed has been with for the last twenty years or so is called the

House Rockers. They have performed at the Chicago Blues Festival, which is attended by 100,000–150,000 people. Rasheed can sing tenor, but he is also a baritone singer. He said that he sings like he makes love. Somebody else might be better than him, but he doesn't think about that when he is doing what he does.

22

THANK YOU MR. KING...THE KING OF THE BLUES

By Dr. C. Sade Turnipseed

I n so many ways, I honor and respect the amazing Mr. Riley "B.B." King. Born in a cabin on a cotton plantation outside Berclair, Mississippi, in 1925, his entire life—much like the lives of so many others from the Mississippi Delta—was spent in service to others. Unfortunately for most of his contemporaries, colleagues and family of friends, they never received the accolades, appreciation or respect for their lifelong work as cotton pickers in the American South. In an effort to do something to heal the pain of neglect, Mr. B.B. King joined the campaign to gather cotton-related stories, artifacts and archival material for the establishment of a monument in tribute to the people he knew best.

Our theory is that the perceptions of sharecropping, tenant farming, etc. will change in significant ways when the memories of these hardworking people are gathered and respectfully shared in the manner they deserve. Mr. King, along with Dr. Maya Angelou, Ed Dwight, Reverend David Matthews, Mississippi congressman Bennie Thompson, Mississippi senator Thad Cochran, National Parks director Dr. Jon Jarvis, Mr. Theodore Turnipseed Sr. and millions of others, understand the importance of sharing and erecting a statue and national park dedicated to the countless field workers of the American South. Though unrecognized and unappreciated, these people worked from sunup to sundown, tilling, planting, chopping, picking and spinning cotton in the blazing hot sun. This, and many other horrifying conditions of the historic South, is what evoked the music we call the blues.

B.B. King and C.
Sade Turnipseed
in Indianola,
Mississippi. *Courtesy of*
C. Sade Turnipseed.

On May 21, 2014, during the last year of his life, Mr. B.B. King accepted our call to become the honorary chair of Khafre Incorporated, a Mississippi-based 501(3) not-for-profit organization. In so doing, he replaced the late Dr. Maya Angelou as the honorary chair of the Cotton Pickers of America and the Sharecroppers Interpretive Center project. The plan is to build a thirty-foot-high monument on twenty acres of cotton land along Highway 61, just outside the historic black town of Mound Bayou, Mississippi. This is a historically rare opportunity to transform many lives in the Delta and engage conversations about race and social inequities in the United States. Our goal is to honor the legacy of the cotton pickers and to say thank you for making blues, like cotton, a global empire.

Blues…like cotton connected the Delta to the whole world.

On behalf of Khafre Incorporated and all the Cotton Pickers of America, I thank you, sir.

Professor C. Sade Turnipseed is the executive director of Khafre Incorporated and teaches American History at Mississippi Valley State University in Itta Bena, the birthplace of Mr. B.B. King. For more information about the Cotton Pickers of America Monument project, please contact her at 662.347.8198, sade@khafreinc.org or www.khafreinc.org.

Conclusion

INFLUENTIAL CONSIDERATIONS ON BLACK MUSIC

The poet Kalamu ya Salaam wrote an article in the *African American Review* titled "It Didn't Jes Grew: The Social and Aesthetic Significance of African American Music." In the article he writes, "Our music is our Mother Tongue, our meta-language that we use for the fullest expression of self." He calls it Great Black Music. He quotes Franklin Rosemont's *Blues and the Poetic Spirit*, which says,

> *American black music originated in the culture of the slaves who were systematically deprived of the more "refined" instruments of human expression....Thus the spoken word, the chant, and dancing were the only vehicles of creative expression left to the slaves. The sublimative energies that in different conditions would doubtless have gone into writing, painting, sculpting, etc., were necessarily concentrated in the naked word and the naked gesture—in the field hollers, work-songs, and their accompanying rhythmic movements—in which gestated the embryo that would eventually emerge as the blues. Black music developed out of, and later side by side with, the vigorous oral poetry combined with dancing, both nourished in the tropical tempest of black magic and the overwhelming desire for freedom.*

Angela Y. Davis, in *Blues Legacies and Black Feminism: Gertrude "Ma" Rainey, Bessie Smith, and Billie Holiday*, says,

> *The blues...the predominant postslavery African American musical form, articulated a new valuation of individual emotional needs and desires. The birth of the blues was aesthetic evidence of new psychosocial realities*

within the black population….Emerging during the decades following the abolition of slavery, the blues gave musical expression to the new social and sexual realities encountered by African Americans as free women and men.

LeRoi Jones (Amiri Baraka) believed that the blues was a personal history of his people in the United States. In his book *Blues People: Negro Music in White America*, he wrote about the types of music that date back to the slaves and brings the history forward into the 1960s. His perspective, written more than fifty years ago, reflected on the influence of Negro music in America.

Kalamu ya Salaam, Angela Y. Davis and Amiri Baraka wrote influential considerations on black music, literature and poetry. These three voices, without a doubt, echo what we all have come to know: the blues music of black America is poetic in the manner that it causes the listener to reflect on a moment, place, time, person and feeling that is central to an individual's experience.

B.B. King laid the blues out on the proverbial red carpet. He did so with integrity, and he succeeded not only in entertaining the world with soulful rhythms but also in educating and inviting us to join in a legacy that will remain in our hearts and minds. As this era passes on to the next generation, let's remember the King for who he was: a kind man, generous to one and all and a true ambassador of his life's work—blues music.

Above and opposite, top: B.B. King receives an honorary doctorate from Mississippi Valley State University in 2002. *Courtesy of Ralph Smith.*

Riley B. King's wreath. *Courtesy of Glynn Fought.*

Bell Grove Missionary Baptist Church in Indianola, Mississippi, where B.B. King's funeral took place. *Courtesy of Diane Williams.*

Governor Phil Bryant at B.B. King's funeral. *Courtesy of Glynn Fought.*

Swiss pianist Silvan Zingg and Diane Williams at B.B. King's funeral in Indianola, Mississippi. *Courtesy of Glynn Fought.*

King's funeral procession in Indianola, Mississippi. *Courtesy of Glynn Fought.*

Burial site—May 30, 2015. *Courtesy of Glynn Fought.*

King's funeral hearse in Indianola, Mississippi. *Courtesy of Glynn Fought.*

King's guitar, Lucille, on a horse on the day of King's funeral in Indianola, Mississippi. *Courtesy of Glynn Fought.*

BLUES CURRICULA

B.B. KING MUSEUM AND DELTA INTERPRETIVE CENTER BLUES CURRICULUM

Indianola, Mississippi, a small town in the Mississippi Delta, is home to the B.B. King Museum and Delta Interpretive Center. Located near King's birthplace, it celebrates the life and work of the man who is known the world over as the King of the Blues. The exhibit space of this state-of-the-art facility contains hundreds of artifacts, most of which were collected and donated by B.B. King himself. Walking through the exhibits is a virtual walk through the history of blues music and includes a generous serving of United States history. There is much to be learned from B.B. King's life and music. Therefore, the museum engaged a music educator to develop a curriculum to be shared and accessed via the museum's website.

The curriculum will assist teachers in introducing their students to B.B. King and blues music. It includes documentary videos, music videos, photographs and other resources that bring the man and his music to life within a classroom. Lessons were created for three grade clusters: Grades four and five, six through eight and nine through twelve.

Each lesson is designed to be taught over two or more days. Lessons are organized around a big idea and are aligned with standards in various subjects, including the visual and performing arts. While the lessons may be taught individually or sequentially, the design of the curriculum exposes students to:

- The life and times of B.B. King, a biographical overview
- B.B. King, King of the Blues, an examination of blues music and lyrics
- A world-class musician, whose collected artifacts represent life and times in America

Lessons in the curriculum engage students through the use of:

- Technology: videos, audio samples, photographs and a slide show
- Interactive small-group tasks, discussions, reporting and presenting
- Large and small group reflections
- Writing prompts for all grades
- Reader's theater, grades six through twelve

Each lesson includes multiple teacher and student resources, some of which include:

- Articles, short biographies, vocabulary words, charts, guides and timelines
- Forty-four still photographs
- Song lyrics to accompany video performances
- Student handout pages
- Group task materials and rubric, grades nine through twelve
- Lesson extensions and suggested assessments

The B.B. King Museum and Delta Interpretive Center Education Curriculum website link is http://www.bbkingmuseum.org/teacher-resources.

Althea Jerome, creator of the B.B. King Museum and Delta Interpretive Center Education Curriculum, is a musician with more than thirty-five years of teaching experience. She holds a Bachelor of Music Education degree from the University of North Texas and a Master of Music Education degree from the University of Southern Mississippi. She has taught music at all grade levels, as well as undergraduate and graduate voice and teacher education courses at the University of Southern Mississippi. With work experience in K-12 public schools, university, community arts organizations and statewide arts and education organizations, she has continuously pursued the importance of arts learning. She has worked as a teaching artist since 2001 and has received training from the Mississippi Arts Commission and the John F. Kennedy Center for the Performing Arts. She offers demonstration lessons focused on arts integration and leads professional development for teachers. Her work as a teaching artist emphasizes arts integration by bringing music and other art forms into all content areas. Since 2001, she has been listed in the Mississippi Arts Commission's Teaching Artist Roster. For the past six years, she has served as a scholar and storyteller in the PrimeTime family literacy program of the Mississippi Humanities Council. In 2015, she was selected to teach a five-day arts residency at two schools in Mississippi as part of a project sponsored by the Mississippi Alliance for Arts Education. In 2012, Althea was a recipient of the Governor's Arts Award for her work in Arts Education.

The Mississippi Blues Trail and Beyond Curriculum

Signs welcoming visitors as they cross the state line into Mississippi indicate that the Magnolia State is the birthplace of America's music. Indeed, many styles of music have emerged along with the historical development of the state that are directly related to social studies, geography, economics, politics, civil rights and media, yet this rich heritage is quite removed from the cognizance of young people living in the twenty-first century. Inculcating elementary students as to the significance, historical value, artistic creativity and psychological/cathartic release of blues music seems to be a perfect place to begin to build perception of the human art form known as the blues.

Conceived in 2012, and awarded a grant from the National Endowment for the Arts, The Mississippi Blues Trail and Beyond is a collaboration of efforts from Mary Margaret Miller White, formerly Heritage Director for the Mississippi Arts Commission; Scott Barretta, blues historian and sociology professor at the University of Mississippi; and Mark Malone, professor of music at William Carey University. Originally designed as a curriculum geared toward fourth-grade students, the material is versatile and may be easily adapted for middle school and high school learners. Six units each contain three detailed lesson plans for implementation by instructors that include: National Arts Standards (music, theater and visual arts), Common Core state standards, Mississippi State Framework for Social Studies (history and geography), behavioral objectives, procedures, materials, formative and summative assessment (both written and performance-based), technology, remedial work, enrichment and accommodations.

B.B. King markers include Itta Bena (Mississippi Delta) and Kilmichael (Mississippi Hills).

Unit I: Music
  Lesson 1: Blues Basics
  Lesson 2: Singing and Playing the Blues
  Lesson 3: Instruments of the Blues

Unit II: Meaning of the Blues
  Lesson 1: Themes of the Blues
  Lesson 2: Emotions of the Blues
  Lesson 3: Women of the Blues

Unit III: Cotton's Effect on the Blues
  Lesson 1: Geography of Mississippi
  Lesson 2: Vocabulary
  Lesson 3: Migration

Unit IV: Transportation and the Blues
  Lesson 1: The Mississippi River
  Lesson 2: Trains
  Lesson 3: Highways and Automobiles

Unit V: Civil Rights
  Lesson 1: General Complaints
  Lesson 2: Political Lyrics
  Lesson 3: Civil Rights Movement

Unit VI: Media and the Blues
  Lesson 1: Early Years of the Blues
  Lesson 2: Recording the Blues
  Lesson 3: Radio and the Blues

Appendix
  I. Materials
  II. Media Resources
  III. Additional Resources

The entire Blues Trail Curriculum may be accessed online by following these steps:
1. Go to the Mississippi Arts Commission website: http://www.arts.state.ms.us/
2. Click on Special Projects and Initiatives
3. Click on Blues Trail Curriculum
4. Click on Sign Up and Download the Curriculum Now
5. Complete the required fields to register to use the information
6. Submit information by clicking Download the Blues Trail Curriculum

Teachers may access recorded teaching assistance with many of the music activities found in Unit I.

Everyone is enthusiastically encouraged to explore the Mississippi Blues Trail Curriculum to encounter the musicians who created, performed and perfected the blues. Along the way, expect to learn an arts-integrated approach to geography, social studies and economics through the lens of the Blues Trail, and thereby discover the untold stories of Mississippi history that are rooted in blues music. Each willing pupil will learn to play blues scales and chords en route to creating original blues music within a historical and social context. As we say in Mississippi, "Y'all come!"

Mark Hugh Malone, PhD
Mississippi Blues Trail Curriculum creator
Professor of music and coordinator of music education
The Winters School of Music
William Carey University
Hattiesburg, Mississippi

B.B. KING DISCOGRAPHY

ALBUMS

Singin' the Blues (1956)
The Blues (1958)
B.B. King Wails (1959)
The Great B.B. King (1960)
King of the Blues (1960)
My Kind of Blues (1961)
More B.B. King (1961)
Easy Listening Blues (1962)
Going Home (1963)
Mr. Blues (1963)
Live at the Regal: Blues Is King (1965)
B.B. King Sings Spirituals (1965)
Better Than Ever (1966)
Confessin' the Blues (1966)
The Kings' Jam (Live Bootleg) with Jimi Hendrix Live from the Generation Club, NY (1967)
Blues on Top of Blues (1968)
Lucille (1968)
Live and Well (1969)
Completely Well (1969)
The Incredible Soul of B.B. King (1970)
Indianola Mississippi Seeds (1970)
A Heart Full of Blues (1970)

Swing Low Sweet Chariot (1970)
I Love You So (1970)
Blues for Me (1970)
Live in Cook County Jail (1971)
B.B. King in London (1971)
L.A. Midnight (1972)
Guess Who (1972)
To Know You Is to Love You (1973)
Friends (1974)
B.B. King and Bobby Bland Together for the First Time: Live (1974)
Bobby Bland and B.B. King Together Again: Live (1976)
King Size (1977)
Midnight Believer (1978)
Take It Home (1979)
Now Appearing at Ole Miss (1980)
There Must Be A Better World Somewhere (1981)
Royal Jam: Live in London (1982)
Love Me Tender (1982)
Blues 'N' Jazz (1983)
Six Silver Strings (1985)
King of the Blues 1989 (1989)
B.B. King and Sons Live: Live at San Quentin (1990)
Live at the Apollo (1991)
There Is Always One More Time (1991)
Blues Summit (1993)
Lucille and Friends (1995)
Deuces Wild (1997)
Blues on the Bayou (1998)
Live in Japan (1999)
Let the Good Times Roll (1999)
Riding with the King (2000)
Making Love Is Good for You (2000)
A Christmas Celebration of Home (2001)
Reflections (2003)
Forever Gold: B.B. King Live (2007)
B.B. King and Friends: 80 (2005)
One Kind Favor (2008)
Live at the BBC (2008)
Live at the Royal Albert Hall 2011 (2012)

ALBUM COMPILATIONS FROM PREVIOUS HITS (1968–2012)

His Best—The Electric B.B. King (1968)
The Best of B.B. King (1973)
Lucille Talks Back (1975)
Why I Sing the Blues (1983)
Do the Boogie! B.B. King's Early '50s Classics (1988)
King of the Blues (1992)
My Sweet Little Angel (1992)
Lucille & Friends (1995)
Greatest Hits (1995)
His Definitive Greatest Hits (1999)
The Ultimate Collection (2005)
The Best of the Early Years (2007)
Legends: B.B. King (2012)

RECORD SINGLES

1949
"Miss Martha King"
"Got the Blues"

1950
"Mistreated Woman"
"I Am"
"My Baby's Gone"

1951
"B.B. Blues"
"She's a Mean Woman"
"3 O'clock Blues"

1952
"Fine-Looking Woman"
"Shake It Up and Go"
"Someday, Somewhere"

"You Didn't Want Me"
"You Know I Love You"
"Story from My Heart and Soul"

1953
"Woke Up this Morning"
"Please Love Me"
"Neighborhood Affair"
"Why Did You Leave Me"
"Please Hurry Home"
"Praying to the Lord"

1954
"The Woman I Love"
"Everything I Do Is Wrong"
"When My Heart Beats Like a Hammer"
"You Upset Me Baby"

1955
"Sneaking Around"
"Every Day I Have the Blues"
"Lonely and Blue"
"Shut Your Mouth"
"Talkin' the Blues"
"What Can't I Do—Just Sing the Blues"
"Ten Long Years"

1956
"Dark Is the Night, Pts. 1 and 2"
"Sweet Little Angel"
"Bad Luck #6"
"On My Word of Honor"

1957
"Early in the Morning"
"How Do I Love You"
"I Want to Get Married"
"Troubles, Troubles, Troubles #7"
"(I'm Gonna) Quit My Baby"

"Be Careful with a Fool #8"
"The Key to My Kingdom"
"Why Do Things Happen to Me"

1958
"Don't Look Now, But You Got the Blues"
"Please Accept My Love"
"You've Been an Angel #9"
"The Fool"

1959
"A Lonely Lover's Plea"
"Time to Say Goodbye"
"Sugar Mama"
"Army of the Lord"

1960
"Sweet Sixteen, Pt. 1"
"Walking Dr. Bill"
"Things Are Not the Same"
"Bad Luck Soul"
"Hold That Train"

1961
"Someday"
"Peace of Mind #10"
"Bad Case of Love"

1962
"My Sometime Baby"
"I'm Gonna Sit till You Give In"
"Down Now"

1963
"The Road I Travel"
"The Letter"
"Precious Lord"

1964
"How Blue Can You Get"
"You're Gonna Miss Me"
"Help the Poor"
"The Worst Thing in My Life"
"Rock Me Baby"
"The Hurt"
"Never Trust a Woman"
"Please Send Me Someone to Love"
"Night Owl"

1965
"I Need You"
"All Over Again"
"I'd Rather Drink Muddy Water"
"Blue Shadows"
"Just a Dream"
"You're Still a Square"
"Broken Promise"

1966
"Eyesight to the Blind"
"Five Long Years"
"Ain't Nobody's Business"
"Don't Answer the Door, Pt. 1"
"I Stay in the Mood"
"Waitin' for You"

1967
"It's a Mean World"
"The Jungle"
"Growing Old"

1968
"Blues for Me"
"I Don't Want You Cuttin' Off Your Hair"
"Shoutin' the Blues"
"Paying the Cost to Be the Boss"
"I'm Gonna Do What They Do to Me"

"The B.B. Jones"
"You Put It on Me #12"
"The Woman I Love"

1969
"Get Myself Somebody"
"I Want You So Bad"
"Get Off My Back Woman #13"
"Why I Sing the Blues"
"Just a Little Love"

1970
"The Thrill Is Gone"
"So Excited"
"Hummingbird"
"Worried Life"
"Ask Me No Questions"
"Chains and Things"

1971
"Nobody Loves Me but My Mother"
"Help the Poor" (re-recording)
"Ghetto Woman"
"The Evil Child"

1972
"Sweet Sixteen" (re-recording)
"I Got Some Help I Don't Need"
"Ain't Nobody Home"
"Guess Who"

1973
"To Know You Is to Love You"

1974
"I Like to Live the Love"
"Who Are You"
"Philadelphia"

1975
"My Song"

1975/1976
"Friends #14"

1976
"Let the Good Times Roll"

1977
"Slow and Easy"

1978
"Never Make a Move Too Soon"

1979
"Better Not Look Down"

1981
"There Must Be a Better World Somewhere"

1985
"Into the Night"

1988
"When Love Comes to Town" with U2

1992
"The Blues Come Over Me"
"Since I Met You Baby" with Gary Moore

2000
"Riding with the King" with Eric Clapton

AWARDS AND DISTINCTIONS

Entertainer of the Year (1980)
Blues Hall of Fame, Blues Foundation—First Inductee

Entertainer of the Year (1981)
Blues Hall of Fame, Blues Foundation
Live Album (1983)
Live at the Regal
Blues Hall of Fame, Blues Foundation

The Thrill Is Gone (1985)
Blues Hall of Fame, Blues Foundation

Rock and Roll Hall of Fame (1987)

Best Video from a Film (1989)
"When Love Comes to Town" with U2
MTV Music Video Awards

Hollywood Walk of Fame (1990)

Band of the Year (1991)
The Handys
The Blues Foundation

Contemporary Blues Album of the Year (1994)
Blues Summit—B.B. King
Handy Blues Award, The Blues Foundation

Keeping the Blues Alive Award (1997)
Blues All Around Me with David Ritz
Blues Foundation

Lifetime Achievement Award (1998)
The MOBO Organization

Blues Album of the Year (1999)
Blues on the Bayou
Handy Blues Awards, The Blues Foundation

Contemporary Blues Album of the Year (2001)
Riding with the King with Eric Clapton
Handy Blues Awards, The Blues Foundation

The Polar Music Prize (2004)
Laureate of Popular Music

Blues Entertainer of the Year (2005, 2004, 2003, 2002, 2001 and 2000)
The Handy Blues Awards, The Blues Foundation

Male Artist of the Year (2006)
Blues Music Awards, The Blues Foundation

Male Artist of the Year (2009)
Blues Music Awards, The Blues Foundation

Album of the Year (2009)
One Kind of Favor
The Blues Foundation

Downbeat Music Magazine Hall of Fame Award (2014)

THE RECORDING ACADEMY

Grammy Awards

Best R & B Vocal Performance—Male (1971)
"The Thrill Is Gone"

Best Ethnic or Traditional Recording (1982)
There Must Be a Better World Somewhere

Best Traditional Blues Recording (1984)
Blues 'N' Jazz

Best Traditional Blues Recording (1986)
"My Guitar Sings the Blues"

Best Traditional Blues Recording (1991)
Live at San Quentin

Best Traditional Blues Album (1992)
Live at the Apollo

Best Traditional Blues Album (1994)
Blues Summit

Best Rock Instrumental Performance (1997)
"SRV Shuffle" with Eric Clapton, Buddy Guy and Bonnie Raitt

Best Traditional Blues Album (2000)
Blues on the Bayou

Best Traditional Blues Album (2001)
Riding with the King with Eric Clapton

Best Pop Collaboration with Vocals (2001)
"Is You Is, Or Is You Ain't My Baby" with Dr. John

Best Traditional Blues Album (2003)
A Christmas Celebration of Hope

Best Pop Instrumental Performance (2003)
"Auld Lang Syne"

Best Traditional Blues Album (2006)
80

Best Traditional Blues Album (2009)
One Kind Favor

Grammy Nominations

Best Contemporary Blues Recording (1988)
"Standing on the Edge of Love" from *The Color of Money* soundtrack

Best Rock Vocal Performance by a Duo or Group (1990)
"When Love Comes to Town" with U2

Best Contemporary Blues Recording (1990)
King of the Blues: 1989

Best Country Vocal Collaboration (1991)
"Waiting on the Light to Change" with Randy Travis

Best Contemporary Blues Recording (1991)
Red Hot + Blue with Lee Atwater

Best Contemporary Blues Album (1999)
Deuces Wild

Best Traditional Blues Album (2001)
Let the Good Times Roll: The Music of Louis Jordan

Best Traditional R & B Vocal Performance (2005)
"Sinner's Prayer" with Ray Charles

CIVIC CITATIONS AND SPECIAL COMMENDATIONS

B'nai Brith Humanitarian Award from Music and Performance Lodge of New York (1973)

Honorary Doctorate from Tougaloo College, Mississippi (1973)

Honorary Doctorate from Yale University (1977)

Honorary Doctorate from Boston Berklee College of Music (1985)

Honorary Doctorate from Rhodes College of Memphis (1990)

National Heritage Award from National Endowment for the Arts (1991)

Award of Distinction from University of Mississippi (1992)

World Music Artist from Blues Summit NAACP (1994)

Kennedy Center Honors Award for Outstanding Contribution to American Culture through the Performing Arts (1995)

Inductee into the NAACP Image Awards Hall of Fame (1999) (referenced in a NAACP statement upon the passing of B.B. King)

Honorary Doctorate from Mississippi Valley State University (2002)

Polar Prize for Music presented by King Carl XVI Gustaf of Sweden (2004)

Mississippi House and Senate Approves Favorite Son Resolution for B.B. King Day (2005)

Governor's Award for Lifetime Achievement in the Arts from Mississippi Arts Commission (2005)

Medal of Freedom presented by President George W. Bush (2006)

Honorary Doctorate from Brown University (2007)

Tennessee Governor's Award (2015)

BIBLIOGRAPHY

Printed Materials

"B.B. King: The Life of Riley." Timeline. PBS: American Masters. 2016. http://www.pbs.org.

Brewer, Jon. *B.B. King: The Life of Riley: Survival is a Word…This Is Its Story.* N.p.: Ovolo Publishing, 2015.

Cheseborough, Steve. *Blues Traveling: The Holy Sites of Delta Blues.* Jackson: University Press of Mississippi, 2001.

Conforth, Bruce Michael, PhD., "Ike Zimmerman: The X in Robert Johnson's Crossroads." Program in American Culture paper, University of Michigan, 2008. http://www.academia.edu.

Dahl, Eric E. *B.B. King's Lucille and the Loves before Her: A Musical Journey through B.B. King's Guitars and Music Gear from His Youth through Today.* Minneapolis, MN: Blue Book Publications, 2013.

Danchin, Sebastian. *Blues Boy: The Life and Music of B.B. King.* Jackson: University Press of Mississippi, 1998.

Drozdowski, Ted. "B.B. King Talks About Living His Songs, Sleeping with the Lights on, and Why You'll Never Catch Him On-Stage in Jeans." *Gibson* (news-lifestyle). April 28, 2008. www.gibson.com.

Gordon, Robert. *Can't Be Satisfied: The Life and Times of Muddy Waters.* Boston: Little Brown and Company, 2002.

Grimm, R.B. *B.B. King Unauthorized and Uncensored.* All ages deluxe edition with videos. N.p.: Famous People Collection, 2013. Kindle.

Harvard University. "Blues Is King: Tribute to B.B. King." Harvard at Home. http://isites.harvard.edu. (site discontinued).

Hirshey, Gerri. "On the Bus with B.B. King." *Rolling Stone*. December 24, 1998. https://www.rollingstone.com.

Keil, Charles. *Urban Blues*. Chicago: University of Chicago Press, 1992.

King, B.B., and David Ritz. *B.B. King Omin Sanoin: Every Day I Have the Blues*. Helsinki, Finland: Johnny Kniga 2003.

———. *Blues All around Me: The Autobiography of B.B. King*. New York: Avon, 1996.

King, B.B., and Dick Waterman. *The B.B. King Treasures: Photos, Mementos and Music from B.B. King's Collection*. New York: Bulfinch, 2005.

Kostelanetz, Richard. *The B.B. King Companion: Five Decades of Commentary*. New York: Schirmer Books, 1997.

Krull, Brian. *Lil' Choo-Choo Johnson, Bluesman*. Indianapolis, IN: Dog Ear Publishing, 2010.

McGee, David. *B.B. King: There Is Always One More Time*. San Francisco, CA: Backbeat Books, 2009.

Nazel, Joseph. *B.B. King: King of the Blues*. Black American Series. Los Angeles: Melrose Square, 1998.

Peek, Philip M., and Kwesi Yankah, eds. *African Folklore: An Encyclopedia*. New York: Routledge, 2004.

Sawyer, Charles. *The Arrival of B.B. King: The Authorized Biography*. New York: Doubleday, 1980.

———. "Riley B. King—A Timeline Project." B.B. King Museum. www.bbkingmuseum.org.

Shirley, David. *Every Day I Sing the Blues: The Story of B.B. King*. New York: F. Watts, 1995.

Walton, Daniel. *B.B. King 58 Success Facts: Everything You Need to Know about B.B. King*. Self-published, Kindle, 2014.

Videos and Documentaries

B.B. King and the Guitar Legends. Blueline Studio, 1991, 2015. DVD.

B.B. King: Blues Summit Live at the B.B. King Blues Club, Memphis, Tennessee. Santa Monica, CA: Universal Music, 2000.

B.B. King: Live at Nick's. West Long Branch, NJ: White Star, 2002. DVD.

B.B. King: Live at the Apollo. Victoria, Australia: Umbrella Entertainment, 2003. DVD.

B.B. King: Living Legend. Stars of Jazz, 2007. DVD.

B.B. King: Standing Room Only. 1990; Sherman Oaks, CA: S'more Entertainment, 2007. DVD.

Brewer, Jon, dir. *B.B. King Live at the Royal Albert Hall 2011*. Bounce Productions, 2012. DVD.

———. *B.B. King: The Life of Riley*. Pottstown, PA: MVD Visual, 2014. DVD.

Dollarhide, Jim, producer. *Life of a Legend*. The B.B. King Museums Films, 2008. DVD.

Eberhardt, Allie, dir. *B.B. King: Blues Master*. Los Angeles: Alfred Music, 2002. DVD.

Ferla, Michel, dir. *B.B. King: Live at Montreux*. Paris: Eagle Rock Entertainment, 1993. DVD

Fuqua, Antoine. *Lightning in a Bottle: A One Night History of the Blues*. Hollywood, CA: Sony Pictures Classic, 2004. DVD.

Gast, Leon, dir. *B.B. King: Live in Africa*. Los Angeles: Shout Factory, 2009. DVD.

James Brown and B.B. King: One Special Night. 1985; Marina Del Rey, CA: Trinity Home Entertainment, 2007. DVD.

Jordan, Lawrence, dir. *B.B. King: Live by Request*. A&E TV Movie, 2003. DVD.

Landis, Jon, dir. *Blues Brothers*. Universal City, CA: Universal Home Video, 1998. DVD.

Les Paul: Chasing Sound. PBS Series. Toronto, Canada: Entertainment One, 2007. DVD.

Martin Scorsese Presents: The Blues: A Musical Journey. PBS Series. Vulcan, 2002. DVD.

Thomas, Joe, dir. *B.B. King: Live*. Los Angeles: Image Entertainment, 2009. DVD.

When Love Comes to Town: B.B. King and U2. Zycopolis Productions, 2013. DVD.

ABOUT THE AUTHOR

D iane Williams calls herself a narratologist. She is a professional performing artist/storyteller, teaching artist, author, poet and mixed media fiber artist, whose tapestries often tells stories. She is a former board chair for the National Storytelling Network and a former board member and life member of the National Association of Black Storytellers. She is a recipient of the Zora Neale Hurston Award and the Oracle Award for Regional Leadership and Service in Storytelling. Three of the books she either authored or edited have won Storytelling World Awards. She is retired from a position in state government as director of grants for the Mississippi Arts Commission. Her writing is included in anthologies and literary journals, and her fiber arts have been included on the cover of literary journals. Diane is currently on the Mississippi Humanities Council Speakers Bureau. She is also a member of the Craftsmen's Guild of Mississippi, and her artwork has been exhibited and lives in the collection of museums. She has exhibited in galleries and artistic and community venues around the region.